'Wise and real, this book by Sharon .... recovery as a doctor and a patient. It's .... helpful resource for those with severe ....
Emma Scrivener, author of *A New Name: Grace and healing for anorexia*

'*Tending to My Thoughts* is a book that needs to be read by every pastor. It not only illuminates the reality of living with severe mental illness, but points to the hope that is found in Jesus, and the ways in which people can experience recovery even when a cure does not come. For fellow sufferers, it provides a wise companion for the journey. Sharon writes with clarity, but more importantly with compassion, and this is a book I will return to time and again.'
Rachael Newham, author and project manager at Kintsugi Hope

'Sharon Hastings has followed up on her powerful testimony *Wrestling with My Thoughts* with a book threaded with realism, practicality and, above all, hope. She never resorts to easy answers nor a pretence of plain sailing in her recovery – she is too vulnerably honest for that. But what she does do is encourage all who read her hard-won words that things can change. A more positive future, even within the darkest constraints of mental illness, is not just possible but available. Thank you, Sharon!'
Mark Meynell, author of *When Darkness Seems My Closest Friend*, preaching trainer and cultural critic

'A unique and brilliant book full of realism and hope. Sharon walks us through her journey of recovery. She speaks with raw honesty, not hiding her failures or glossing over her pain. Recovery is not simply cure, but living a life that is filled with purpose, and even joy, despite battling mental illness. She examines those tools that she has found helpful, looking at them through a Christian lens. I found the last chapter, on our eternal hope, most encouraging. As you read this book you will find yourself engaged with the story and helped by Sharon's wisdom.'
Paul Ritchie, pastor of Limerick Baptist Church and author of *Is It Unspiritual to Be Depressed?*

'Sharon is one of my favourite mental health writers. She is seriously intelligent, deeply practical and disarmingly honest. *Tending to My Thoughts* exhibits the best of her writing in perhaps the most helpful exploration of serious mental illness you will ever read. It combines personal account, expert opinion and vital faith in equal measure. I recommend it unreservedly.'
Revd Will van der Hart, director of Mind and Soul Foundation

At the age of six, Sharon Hastings self-published her first book: *The Long Train Went Under the Bridge*, held together with staples. Writing has always been a big part of her life. She told her teachers she wanted to be an author when she grew up, and that dream never really left her, even when her love of people and her desire to help them drew her towards a career in medicine.

As a medical student, Sharon wrote for magazines and websites, and notably saw her 'History of Gastric Surgery in Belfast' (a collaborative effort with her uncle, a surgeon) published in the *Ulster Medical Journal*. And when poor health got in the way of practising as a doctor, Sharon attended creative writing classes, which was where she met her husband, Robert, a video producer and budding sci-fi author who has become her primary carer and greatest cheerleader.

Despite her struggle with severe mental illness, Sharon graduated with a degree in Medicine and a Certificate in Counselling from Queen's University, Belfast, in 2007. She went on to achieve a Postgraduate Certificate in Clinical Education and briefly taught anatomy at the university before moving into Constituency Casework roles in the offices of three successive elected representatives.

The schizoaffective disorder that first emerged when she was at medical school affects every aspect of Sharon's life, but her faith remains central to her journey. Pastoral support is as important to her as the vital ongoing input from mental health professionals, and in her first book with IVP (2020), *Wrestling with My Thoughts*, she wrote about encountering God in the midst of depression, mania and psychosis.

Sharon enjoys life in County Down with Rob, their young son and two golden retrievers. Her interests include live music, mindfulness practice and outdoor walks. At the time of writing, Sharon is a full-time mum, but her ministry through the written word remains important to her.

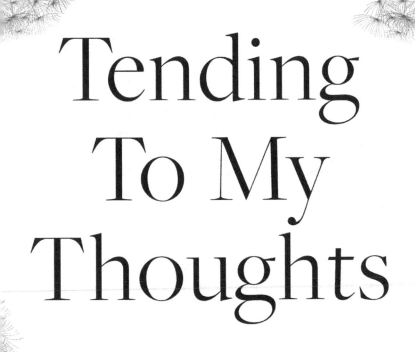

Tending To My Thoughts

SHARON HASTINGS

INTER-VARSITY PRESS
SPCK Group, The Record Hall, 16–16A Baldwin's Gardens, London, EC1N 7RJ
Email: ivp@ivpbooks.com
Website: www.ivpbooks.com

First published 2024

British Library Cataloguing-in-Publication Data
A catalogue record for this book is available from the British Library.

ISBN: 978–1–78974–454–5
eBook ISBN: 978–1–78974–455–2

Set in 11/14pt Minion Pro

Typeset in Great Britain by Fakenham Prepress Solutions, Fakenham, Norfolk

For Claire

For I am convinced that neither death nor life, neither angels
nor demons, neither the present nor the future, nor any powers,
neither height nor depth, nor anything else in all creation, will
be able to separate us from the love of God that is in Christ Jesus
our Lord.
(Romans 8:38–39)

Finally, brothers and sisters, whatever is true, whatever is noble, whatever is right, whatever is pure, whatever is lovely, whatever is admirable – if anything is excellent or praiseworthy – think about such things.
(Philippians 4:8)

The process of living seems to consist in coming to realize truths so ancient and simple that, if stated, they sound like barren platitudes. They cannot sound otherwise to those who have not had the relevant experience: that is why there is no real teaching of such truths possible and every generation starts from scratch.
(C. S. Lewis, *Letters of C. S. Lewis*)[1]

Contents

Preface and acknowledgments

This book follows on from my first memoir, *Wrestling with My Thoughts: A doctor with severe mental illness discovers strength*, in which I shared my struggle with schizoaffective disorder and my realisation that – whatever I go through – God is good, he holds me in his right hand, and he gives me strength.

In 2018, when I wrote *Wrestling with My Thoughts*, I was still very unwell. I thought that God had purposed for me to live for him in the context of ongoing illness. Today, I believe that God has more for me. This book picks up the story at the point at which I began to ask whether recovery might actually be possible. It details my progress to the present day, when I can say that my life is no longer constantly dominated by mental illness.

As in *Wrestling with My Thoughts*, I have tried to ensure that I do not tell anyone else's story. Names and identifying features of mental health professionals and some others have been changed. I could have written a lot more about my journey as a mum, but I want our son to be able to tell his own story when he is of an age to do so. If he features less in the book than might be expected, it is because I want to respect his right to privacy.

Everything I have written about actually happened. In some vignettes I have included dialogue, and this is recorded to the best of my memory, holding to the spirit of what was actually said. The medical details included are correct at the time of writing.

The goal of this book is to generate hope that recovery (not in the sense of 'cure', but of having a life worth living) is possible for almost everyone. I was conscious while writing that recovery may seem like a distant dream to some readers, and have prayed before each writing session that God would inspire me to tell my story honestly and compassionately with that in mind.

In some ways, *Tending to My Thoughts* has required more soul-searching than *Wrestling with My Thoughts*, and has been harder to write. I believe it has been a worthwhile process, at least for me, and I trust that some of the insights I have garnered will be new and helpful to my readers.

Many people continue to help me along my writing journey. With respect to *Tending to My Thoughts*, I would particularly like to acknowledge:

Rob, my husband and fellow writer, for his unrelenting loyalty, for journeying this recovery with me – even as I prove again and again that it is not a linear road – and for being such a great daddy to our little one (who enjoyed some extra father–son time while I was finishing this project).

My parents, for throwing themselves so enthusiastically into their roles as Granny and Pa, for always arriving with a freshly baked loaf under one arm and a bunch of yellow roses under the other, and for bringing me up to know Jesus.

Olivia, for helping to conceive the idea for this book and believing in it – even when its future seemed uncertain, for reminding me to keep putting one foot in front of the other on the most difficult days, and for loving the three of us in practical and intangible ways, week after week after week.

Peter, for infecting me with his passion for living a meaningful and extraordinary life, for casting his eagle eye over my chapters, pointing out inconsistencies and pushing me to make better choices of words, and for his prayerful and wholehearted approach to caring for us as a family.

Gordon and Helen, for injecting our lives with wisdom, love and humour, for being a wonderful example of a godly couple for us to look up to, and for the joy that they take in our little one.

Avril, for being such a constant, sensible, encouraging, praying presence, and the best friend a girl (and her family) could ask for.

My editor at IVP, Thomas Creedy, for choosing the right time to take this project forward, for believing in me as a writer, and for the insights and suggestions, gently shared, which have made this book what it is today.

Our family GP, for helping us navigate pregnancy and early parenthood in a challenging context, for listening to me in times of struggle, and for reminding me that – whatever decisions health-care professionals may make – God is sovereign and can always be trusted.

The 'Hastings Helpers', the team drawn from our church that provided meals, emotional support, prayer and fellowship in the early days after our baby was born, for their commitment and compassion, and for being an extension of our family.

The staff of the South Eastern Health and Social Care Trust Recovery College, for giving me the idea that recovery was possible.

My Sunday school teachers and Every Girl's Rally leaders, for teaching me many Bible stories and memory verses thirty years ago, which come to mind as I write today.

Readers of *Wrestling with My Thoughts*, for the feedback, support and encouragement that inspired me to write more.

Gordon (again), Ken and Stephanie, for their continued support for my writing and for their thoughtful and helpful contributions to this book.

Andrew, our minister, and the leaders of our church, for pastoring and teaching me, and for providing a spiritual home for our family.

Soli Deo Gloria.

Prologue
'What's next for Steve?'

In a training video on the subject of recovery-focused mental healthcare produced by the American Psychiatric Association, Larry Davidson, a psychologist and professor at Yale School of Medicine, speaks about a late colleague, Professor Thomas A. Kirk, who was Commissioner of the Connecticut Department of Mental Health and Addiction Services from 1999 to 2009.

'Tom' liked to spend time in the field, talking to practitioners and patients, and often told the story of Steve, a twenty-seven-year-old man living in a group home [supported living accommodation], which he visited.

Tom had had the opportunity to have a coffee with Steve, and afterwards debriefed with the staff. 'How's Steve doing?' he asked.

They replied, 'He's great! He's become a model patient . . . settled in really well and hasn't been back to the hospital, takes his medicine without any fuss, goes to all his groups – he's just terrific!'

'That's really great,' Tom replied. 'It's a credit to you; it's a credit to Steve. So, tell me, what's next for Steve?'

'What do you mean, what's next for Steve?' came their reply. 'He's become a model patient . . . He's doing what he's supposed to be doing.'

'That's great,' said Tom, again. 'So what's next for Steve?'

At this point he asked them to imagine that they were twenty-seven years old and had a serious mental illness, and they were going to their groups and taking their medication and being a model patient at their group home. Would that be all they would want out of life?[1]

Professor Davidson notes: 'The lesson from this story is that people with mental illnesses typically want the same things out of their life as other people do. People are not their diagnoses . . . In the past, the mental health system has addressed illness and its symptoms, and not the person and his or her everyday life.'

In mental healthcare, the recovery model seeks to ensure that there is hope of a meaningful life beyond illness for people like Steve . . . and like me. This is my story of finding recovery through tending to my thoughts.

Introduction

'Darkness is my closest friend.'
(Psalm 88:18)

Downe Hospital Acute Mental Health Inpatient Unit (2016)

'Shh! Shh! Shhhh!' My whisper is barely audible, but my lips tremble and my head shakes. 'Stop it!' But they don't. The flapping gets stronger; the network is active.

I lean my head forward into my right elbow and exhale sharply, pulling my hoodie further over my head with my left hand. The chair I'm sitting on feels hard and cold. I face the corner, rocking backwards and forwards.

'Sharon?'

I hear a soft voice behind me, but I don't turn round.

'The teas will be out in a moment.'

The shutter on the kitchen hatch rattles. I hunch myself up small, rounding my shoulders and hugging my knees.

'Will I bring you one?'

The voice is louder this time, closer to my ear. I shudder, then nod, turning forty-five degrees to the side and then quickly back again.

Clinking mugs. Chatter. Someone shouting about needing their phone charger.

The sounds blur together. My throat is dry.

'It's here, beside you. I've brought you a packet of custard creams – your favourite.'

Hoodie pulled right down to the end of my nose, I slowly turn and reach my hand out to take the drink. I see feet and ankles, slipper socks and scuffed trainers.

Another voice, coarse from smoking. 'D'ye wanna sit with us, Sharon, love?'

1

I hesitate for a second, taking a breath. I want to . . . My hoodie slips up and I catch an eye. Some tea spills over my hand. I gasp. The air is thick with electric transmissions.

'No!' My own voice now, cracking as I crouch back into my corner. I set down my tea, and cup my hands tightly over my ears.

'It must be her voices,' the smoker says to the others, knowingly.

I feel a light tap on my shoulder.

'Sharon, the doctor wants to see you. Are you able to come with me?'

I push my chair back from the corner and shuffle to a standing position – one hand to my head, the other grasping my mug. Barely seeing, I can feel a thousand eyes on me.

There's a dialogue in my head: 'Maybe there's something he can do. . . . ' 'But what if he's one of them?' 'I need help.' 'He might be in on it.' 'Talk to him.' 'Don't say a thing.'

I draw my breath in sharply, then follow the nurse into an interview room.

A decade-long battle . . . and it wasn't over yet

Anxiety, depression, anorexia, mania . . . and the hallucinations and delusions of psychosis.

Antidepressants, anticonvulsants, mood stabilisers, antipsychotics, anxiolytics (in tens of different combinations and dosing regimens) . . . and drugs to treat their side effects.

Community mental health teams, home treatment teams, a day hospital, the Eating Disorder Service, the Early Intervention in Psychosis Service . . . and multiple, prolonged inpatient admissions.

Treatment in Northern Ireland, London and Wickenburg (Arizona, USA).

Cognitive behavioural therapy, psychoanalytic psychotherapy, art therapy . . . and even electroconvulsive therapy (ECT).

A summary of the decade between my twenty-fourth birthday in 2006 and thirty-fourth in 2016 reads like the index of a psychiatry textbook.

During that time, I went from being a reasonably happy and capable senior medical student to an apparently hopeless psychiatric case, passing through a sequence of diagnoses from 'major depressive disorder with eating disorder (not otherwise specified)', through bipolar disorder, and finally to schizoaffective disorder.

At my best, I managed to graduate as a doctor; to work at different stages as an anatomy tutor and as a constituency assistant to a member of the legislative assembly (MLA) in Belfast; and to marry my long-suffering best friend, Rob.

At my worst, I languished in treatment facilities; attempted suicide (at home, in 2009); and found myself, as in the scene described at the start of this Introduction, crippled by paranoid psychosis.

Today (in 2022), I barely recognise that poor, tormented girl in her baggy clothes and with her grey, gaunt face, cowering in the corner of the mental health unit's communal dining area. Yet that was my reality for much of my adult life. (I have written more about this – and about the glimmers of hope that occasionally illuminated my life – in a previous memoir, *Wrestling with My Thoughts* (IVP, 2020).)

I would say that 2016 was, in some ways, the nadir of my mental decline. It was the year in which my inpatient psychiatrist decided to prescribe clozapine, a powerful antipsychotic reserved only for patients whose symptoms have failed to respond to more conventional treatments because of its potentially serious side effects.

It was also the first year I was treated with ECT after I developed some of those side effects and the clozapine had to be stopped. This, too, failed (although I would have two further series of treatments later), and left me with significant memory loss.

Understandably, I felt like giving up; not in the sense of wanting to end my life, but in accepting that I was probably going to be largely institutionalised, sedated and episodically psychotic for the rest of my days. Things such as having a family, working in a meaningful job or participating in the life of my church just seemed like a pipe dream.

Most of all my heart broke for Rob, who had married me at a relative high point, only to see me deteriorate again. Visiting a broken, despairing wife in a psychiatric hospital was hardly what he'd had in mind when he vowed to love me 'in sickness and in health'.

I didn't spend quite the whole year in hospital, however, and while I was at home, something seemingly small and insignificant happened that would pave the way for seismic life change to occur. On a cold and dreary afternoon, in the drab prefab offices of the community mental health team, a nurse asked me if I would like to be referred to a new service that had opened in the local health trust.

'It's called the Recovery College,' she told me, and it ran courses for people with mental illness who wanted to improve their self-management. People like me. I didn't believe for a moment that I was going to recover. I was also convinced that I couldn't possibly manage my illness any better than I was already doing, as it was so very severe that all my efforts seemed ineffective. But I needed something to give me structure and routine, so I agreed to enrol.

Hope deferred . . .

Before I could begin any courses, I found myself in hospital again. Some of the most powerful memories I have of this admission are of a little quiet room in which I was allowed to spend some time alone. It wasn't quite a hospital chapel, but it did have tall, stained-glass windows, and the décor was muted and peaceful.

It was here that I reflected on my situation: how I had married with such a hope for the future, only to find that my schizoaffective disorder really was, as the textbooks say, 'severe and enduring'. At the same time, I had a deep sense of God's love in this place. Sometimes the sunlight would play through the trees behind the coloured glass, creating dancing rainbows on the floor in front of me. I was ill, yet still aware of beauty.

Introduction

My psychosis manifested in the form of evil presences and shadowy creatures all around me. I felt surrounded by dark influences, yet I knew God's holy presence with me. In hospital, I lived a life separate from my community, following a contrived routine alien to my friends. I was isolated, yet conscious of the prayers of fellow Christians. The disciplines of silence and solitude, practised daily in that quiet room, helped to sustain my faith.

And every week, at least once, one of the ministerial team from my church would visit me in the main ward. I sensed that it was a little awkward for them there, seeing me so tormented and vulnerable, yet their compassion as they read from the Bible, if only a single verse or a simple psalm, never failed to touch my broken heart.

I came to believe that, just as Jesus drew the little children to his knee, God had a heart of compassion for those vulnerable adults who, like me, had lost touch with reality.

I yearned for more of his power in my life. In my lucid moments I prayed passionately for his peace and for release from my pain. On days when I was too troubled to find words, I took solace in the words of Romans 8:26, which says that 'the Spirit himself intercedes for us through wordless groans'.

With thoughts of recovery and college courses pushed from my consciousness, I came to a firm conclusion: God had allowed me to suffer this severe and enduring mental illness for a reason. It was my calling to live well as a Christian with schizoaffective disorder. I merely needed to accept my symptoms and seek God's will in the context of enduring illness.

At this time, I had no idea there was a model of recovery that begins with just such an acceptance. I simply felt a release from my striving; a peace that transcended all understanding (see Philippians 4:7).

Tending to My Thoughts is a story of balancing acceptance and change, of healing that does not equate to cure . . . and of eternal hope beyond anything I can imagine – even today – here on earth.

Join me on this journey towards recovery, whether you have severe mental illness, mental ill health, a sense of poor wellbeing or the blessing of good mental health. I believe we are all in recovery from something – if only our own sinfulness – and that, as Christians, we can move forward, confident that God 'who began a good work in [us] will carry it on to completion until the day of Christ Jesus' (Philippians 1:6).

The process of writing my story has been helpful to me; charting the difficulties, but also my progress. I have had to be deeply honest with myself as I seek to be honest with you, my reader. It has not always been comfortable, but I hope that you will find my writing real, and that there will be places where it resonates.

I have used grey boxes to explain some of the medical terminology and concepts I refer to as I go along. I hope these will be enlightening and will help you form a deeper understanding.

At the beginning of each chapter I have highlighted relevant recovery principles.[1] There are ten of these in total, identified by the Substance Abuse and Mental Health Services Administration (SAMHSA) in the US (see grey box on 'Recovery-focused health-care' in chapter 1). I feel they are useful in defining the process of recovery I seek to describe.

My hope is that you will enjoy this book, feel challenged by it, and be inspired to journey forward in your own recovery, whatever that might look like.

What is severe and enduring mental illness?

Since Covid-19 arrived on the world stage – bringing with it lockdowns, homeworking, homeschooling and, for many, months of shielding and isolation – mental health has become an international topic of conversation and concern.

We're encouraged to ask each other, 'How are you coping with it all?' Outdoor wellness groups have sprung up and the mental health of our children is a major consideration when the experts decide whether schools can operate safely.

Given the hushed tones in which we have spoken of mental health for so many years, this can only be a good thing for everyone . . . or can it?

Everyone has mental health, we say – be it good, bad or indifferent – and must tend to it.

This is true, but there is a real risk that one group will end up overlooked here, and that is the 3% of the population suffering from what psychiatrists call 'severe and enduring' mental illness. This category broadly refers to illnesses defined by psychosis: schizophrenia, bipolar disorder and schizoaffective disorder (these individual illnesses are described in the grey boxes that follow).

While symptoms of severe and enduring mental illnesses can often be managed, there is, as yet, no cure. Research suggests that life has also become harder for people with schizophrenia, bipolar disorder and schizoaffective disorder during the pandemic. Many feel that their needs in these circumstances have been forgotten.

We need to be careful that we don't conflate the stress and struggle associated with temporary sets of circumstances with the life-changing, life-limiting and lifelong impacts of severe and enduring mental illness. The pandemic has spotlighted mental health. Let's capitalise on the opportunity to expand our knowledge of mental illness, for understanding is the foundation of the fight against stigma.

Is 'recovery' from severe and enduring mental illness possible? In 2019, I didn't think so.

In 2022, I found new hope . . .

What is schizophrenia?

Schizophrenia is a severe and enduring mental illness that affects the way people think,[2] causing hallucinations and delusions (known as 'positive symptoms'), and making it harder for people to look after themselves because of a loss of motivation or interest ('negative symptoms').

Hallucinations and delusions are symptoms of **psychosis**, which is a loss of touch with reality.[3] A **hallucination** is a perception of something others do not perceive, such as a voice other people can't hear. A **delusion** is a firmly held belief that others understand to be false.

In my psychosis, I perceived an evil presence that I could feel and others couldn't. I saw flapping, pterodactyl-like creatures that were invisible to those around me. I also had a fixed belief that I was party to messages coming through a network in the fourth dimension, and that I was the target of a conspiracy; something I now realise was untrue.

Around 1% of people suffer from schizophrenia. The mainstay of treatment is antipsychotic medication. This is often effective, but can cause side effects such as sedation and weight gain. Antipsychotic drugs are believed to work by suppressing excessive activity of the neurotransmitter dopamine in the brain.[4] Some patients may be offered specific talking therapies as well as drugs.

What is bipolar disorder?

Bipolar disorder is a severe and enduring mental illness that primarily affects people's moods, causing episodes of **mania** (abnormally high mood) and **depression** (low mood).[5] People with bipolar disorder may also experience psychotic symptoms consistent with their mood, for example believing they are a member of the royal family while manic, or that they are dead while depressed.

When I was manic, I dressed flamboyantly and wore brightly coloured makeup. My thoughts raced, and I once wrote an 80,000-word novel in two weeks. I had little need for food or sleep; my speech jumped from one topic to another, becoming unintelligible; and I spent money I did not have.

When I was depressed, I felt as though the whole world had been drained of its colour. My mood was so low that I cried for hours at a time. I believed my life was not worth living; I felt tired and achy; I was physically slowed down, and my face lacked expression; and I lost all appetite.

Around 1–2% of people are diagnosed with bipolar disorder. The mainstay of treatment is mood-stabilising medication, often in combination with antipsychotic drugs. Talking treatments and self-management programmes may also be offered.

What is schizoaffective disorder?

Schizoaffective disorder is a severe and enduring mental illness that affects both mood and thinking. People with schizoaffective disorder suffer from episodes of mania and/or depression, and also from psychosis, which occurs when the person's mood is normal.[6]

I was diagnosed with schizoaffective disorder in 2011, when I had my first episode of psychosis at a time when my mood was neither manic nor depressed. It came as a shock to me, as I had become accustomed to the 'bipolar disorder' diagnosis I had received previously, and I felt that the 'schizo' prefix was very stigmatising.

Schizoaffective disorder affects around 0.5% of people. It is usually managed with a combination of antipsychotic and mood-stabilising drugs. Talking therapies may also form part of the treatment.

At the end of each chapter I have chosen to share some words from the Bible that have been helpful to me at different stages of my recovery, and to reflect on how they have been part of my journey. These sections are titled 'Scripture and reflection'. I have also added two questions to prompt you to reflect on your own journey as you move through the book.

Scripture and reflection

Lord, do not rebuke me in your anger
　or discipline me in your wrath.
Have mercy on me, Lord, for I am faint;
　heal me, Lord, for my bones are in agony.
My soul is in deep anguish.
　How long, Lord, how long?

Turn, Lord, and deliver me;
　save me because of your unfailing love.
Among the dead no one proclaims your name.
　Who praises you from his grave?
I am worn out from my groaning.

All night long I flood my bed with weeping
    and drench my couch with tears.
My eyes grow weak with sorrow;
    they fail because of all my foes.

Away from me, all you who do evil,
    for the LORD has heard my weeping.
The LORD has heard my cry for mercy;
    the LORD accepts my prayer.
All my enemies will be overwhelmed with shame and anguish;
    they will turn back and suddenly be put to shame.
(Psalm 6)

During the 2016 hospital admissions I mentioned earlier, the ministers who visited me often read from Psalms. I was already familiar with many of their words. My late grandmother had loved the psalms, and I often read them aloud to her in the last few years of her life.

It was only at this point, however, that I began to grasp the importance of lament, and to read the psalms of lament as my own prayers. They gave me words when I could muster none of my own, granted me permission to express my deeply felt emotions directly to God and helped me to feel that I was not alone.

One such psalm, number 13, became especially meaningful to me. In it, David wrote of 'wrestling' with his thoughts (13:2), a concept that seemed to capture exactly what I was doing myself as I desperately tried to gain control over thoughts that seemed so overwhelming as to choke me. (*Wrestling with My Thoughts* ultimately became the title of my first memoir.)

In 2016, however, I took the words of Psalm 6, another psalm of David, as my personal lament. I couldn't believe how David's vivid descriptions of his illness so closely mirrored my own, despite our vastly different circumstances. How often in that mental health unit my bedsheets dripped with tears. How my eyes burnt from weeping! How exhausted I felt from groaning. How my very bones ached!

Just as David wrote of his soul's deep anguish, the very essence of my 'self' was in mortal pain. Just as David cried 'How long?', my torturous moments seemed to follow one after another in unending sorrow.

Yet, like David, I did not at this time feel utterly unheard. Somehow I knew, very profoundly, a sense of connection with my Creator. I did not feel that he had abandoned me to this fate; I did not feel that my lament was distasteful to him.

> For the LORD has heard my weeping.
> The LORD has heard my cry for mercy;
>   the LORD accepts my prayer.
> (Psalm 6:8–9)

When someone doesn't just listen but really hears another person in this sense, psychologists call it 'validation'. Karyn Hall PhD defines validation as: 'The recognition and acceptance of another person's thoughts, feelings, sensations and behaviours as understandable.'[7] There is evidence that the experience of being validated is very powerful and may even represent a foundation for recovery from certain mental health conditions. I didn't know this in 2016, but it is a phenomenon I recognise at work in my life today.

If validation from another person has power, how much more powerful is validation from God himself? Knowing that God heard me gave me consolation and a feeling of rest. It may even have planted a seed of hope.

Questions for personal reflection or discussion

1. What is your perception of people with severe mental illness? How do you think God sees such people?
2. Are you aware of anything you need to recover from? Do you feel heard by God?

1
Planting a seed

The recovery college

'The hope of the afflicted will never perish.'
(Psalm 9:18)

Recovery principle 1
'The belief that recovery is real provides the essential and motivating message of a better future – that people can and do overcome the . . . challenges, barriers, and obstacles that confront them.'

Recovery principle 2
'Mutual support . . . including the sharing of experiential knowledge and skills, as well as social learning, play an invaluable role in recovery.'

'Hope is important. If I can't imagine that my life is going to be better, then I stop trying . . . The most important thing we do is engender hope: to give people hope, to remind people of hope, to focus on what people want and give them hope that it can actually be done.'[1]
(Ron Diamond MD, Professor of Psychiatry at the University of Wisconsin and Medical Director of the Mental Health Center of Dane County)

South Eastern Health and Social Care Trust Recovery College (September 2016)

The hill on the way up to the hospital is steep, and the September air thick with moisture. My gloved fingers are damp and cold. I pull up my hood, then take it down again.

The location of the enrolment session seems ironic: a recovery college in the old Downpatrick asylum. I part my lips. Perhaps the repurposing of the building should bring hope. Where once there were hundreds of lifelong residents, only a psychiatric intensive care unit and addictions ward remain. The twenty-six acute inpatient beds are now located on the site of the new General Hospital.

Still, I shiver as I push open the heavy double doors with a paper arrow taped to them, reminded of the other old asylum in Belfast where I had my first psychiatric admission. I trip on frayed carpet.

'Hello.' The girl's face is carefully made up, but her features are warm and open. 'Are you here for the enrolment session? It's just in the second room on the left.'

My shoulders drop a little and I lift the corners of my mouth deliberately, nodding.

The door handle is sticky, but I step through into a long, large room set out as if for a school class, with tables made up of small desks. At the first of these, a dark-haired lady has a list of names and a pile of green A4 books that turn out to be prospectuses.

'Is this your first time to enrol with the recovery college?'

'Yes.' My smile comes a bit more easily this time. I give her my name.

She ticks off 'Sharon Hastings' and hands me a book.

'Help yourself to tea or coffee and have a look at this. The introductory courses start from page six. There'll be a short welcome talk at 10.30.'

Two other people are sitting with prospectuses: a young girl who is twisting her hair around her finger and a middle-aged man with a grey face. Another two women are chatting at the front of the room. I take them to be staff. Helping myself to some strong tea and a shortbread biscuit, I sit down near the emergency exit. A few more people sign in.

At 10.30, one of the ladies at the front opens a PowerPoint presentation and says a few words about the college, talking about how recovery is for all, and how coming here today is the first step for each of us in a journey towards 'hope, control and opportunity'.

I cast a glance sideways. Three weeks post-discharge from my third hospital admission of 2016, it feels as though recovery is for all but Sharon Hastings.

'I'm a peer trainer,' the lady continues, 'which means I have lived experience of mental illness, but now I work in the college and help co-produce our courses with professionals who have learned experience. That's a core principle of the college: co-production. You will always find courses delivered by mental health professionals and your peers with mental health diagnoses.'

I lift my head from my fist, interested. This person is well dressed and composed. I feel drab and disorganised in comparison. My thoughts drift. Memories and flashbacks from the past couple of years – when recovery has seemed so far away – flood my senses.

Suddenly, I realise that the other lady, who seems to be in charge, has taken over and is giving instructions. We are each to meet individually with peer support workers in the next room to set up something called an individual learning plan. They will call each of us in turn. In the meantime, we are encouraged to look again at our prospectuses and highlight anything of particular interest.

I flick through the pages. A course on peer advocacy catches my eye. I met with peer advocates in the inpatient unit and thought at the time that it might be a job I would be suited to, having done constituency work in the past, with a heavy focus on constituent advocacy. It looks like there are prerequisites though – a self-advocacy course, for a start.

A hand taps my shoulder and the girl I first met in the corridor ushers me through to a smaller room. She introduces herself as Lucy.

'I'm here to help you make an ILP – an individual learning plan – for the autumn semester. We're running the course we usually suggest

*people take first – 'What is Recovery?' – next week, if you'd like to
sign up for that.'*

My cheeks are hot. 'Yes, please.'

*A few minutes later, I leave, smiling, with a document showing my
chosen courses: 'What is Recovery?', 'Anxiety Management' and 'Self-
advocacy'. What had my community psychiatric nurse (CPN) said?
That at the very least it would give me some structure.*

*Heading back down the hill, I add an inch to my step. Well, that's
something.*

* * *

I had found the quiet room in the hospital so helpful. I found it
harder to find peace once I was discharged. There were moments
of light, of course. Rob and I went out to the shore every morning
with our two golden retrievers, and I loved capturing the sunrises
with my camera phone. We enjoyed travelling a bit further afield at
the weekends, sometimes having valuable moments of family time,
and we had some lovely quiet evenings listening to music, reading
or watching a series together.

But schizoaffective disorder was very much in the forefront of
our lives. I had improved a little in the ward and had pleaded with
my consultant to let me go home. Once there, I struggled daily with
depression, and walked a precipice between sanity and psychosis.

Spiritually, I was in active relationship with God, laying bare my
heart as the psalms had taught me to do, but I felt as though he
was allowing me to struggle for longer and to a greater extent than
I could bear. I found church very hard, and some of my friendships there fizzled out – mainly through lack of engagement on my
part, but in some cases because my mental baggage was simply too
heavy.

My nurse's offer of referral to a recovery college – a concept that
was entirely new to me – had not really brought me much hope.
It interested me that there were people in mental healthcare who
thought recovery was possible, but I didn't think anyone would
believe it could be possible for me.

When I enrolled for 'What is Recovery?' in the autumn of 2016, I did so with little curiosity. I thought I knew what recovery looked like for people with depression or anxiety who had seen good results from drug and talking treatments. I had seen many, many more people like me, features dulled and sallow from anti-psychotics, plodding towards a future where going to a day centre rather than being a long-term inpatient was viewed as a success story.

And I didn't glean much from the course at the time – more because my mind was so closed to the new ideas presented to me than because there was nothing to learn. I heard about things like 'positive steps', 'CHIME factors' (CHIME stands for connected-ness, hope, identity, meaning and empowerment) and 'self-care', but I didn't internalise any of them. Aside from my prejudices and cynicism, my cognitive processes were also hampered by sedative drugs. New ideas were difficult to process.

It was also confusing for me, given that I wasn't making any progress at home. In fact, any coping strategies I had developed were failing and I was not drawing solace from my faith. I found myself phoning my nurse every day to plead for help with low mood, unsettling thoughts and increasing agitation.

Rather than telling me that I could recover, my mental health professionals reinforced my own perceptions of how severely ill I was by beginning to discuss readmission. I was creating an impossible workload for my community nurse, and she reluctantly referred me back to the Home Treatment Team, who could see me every day.

The Home Treatment Team not only offer an alternative to hospital in the community; they also hold the keys to inpatient beds. I desperately wanted to stay at home, but day by day I was becoming more psychotic, plagued by the familiar evil presence and tormentors, and developing increasingly complex delusions involving the network in the fourth dimension.

I clearly remember the day that I was persuaded to take a hospital bed. Rob was at work when I took the daily phone call from the Home Treatment nurse, usually in place to arrange a home visit. I was terrified as I talked on my mobile, feeling that danger lurked everywhere. I was unable to lift my eyes in case I saw the tormentors' shadows.

The male nurse was kind. I told him I wouldn't feel any safer in hospital, but he somehow convinced me that I needed the kind of help the acute inpatient unit could provide. Refusing a taxi, I made my own way to the hospital, muttering to myself as I walked up the last hill.

I remember the ward staff being barely able to conceal their shock at my appearance: dishevelled, skinny and evidently tortured by my own thoughts. I also remember my own feelings of utter brokenness as I realised I had fallen so hard and so fast once again.

But it was not a terribly long admission by past standards. Being in the low-stimulus environment of the ward seemed to help me, and I soon began to look a bit more like myself, gaining a bit of weight and beginning to wear a little makeup again. I practised yoga in my room and ran on the treadmill in the ward gym for half an hour every morning. I looked forward to my lunchtime phone calls and evening visits with Rob.

On the basis that I seemed to become most psychotic when depressed, my psychiatrist added a tiny dose of antidepressant to my drug regimen (something that had previously been avoided because of my history of mania, which can be triggered by antidepressant therapy). Over the next few weeks I grew stronger and saner, and was discharged just before Christmas.

I had kept in contact with the recovery college, letting them know why I couldn't attend my autumn courses. As part of my discharge plan for creating structure once I was at home, I enrolled for more classes in January 2017.

This time, even though I had had very little experience of the college's courses, I had already decided that I wanted to get more involved in this co-production and co-delivery process I had heard about. The first course I took was a three-day series of interactive 'Train the Trainer' seminars, intended for students who wanted to volunteer as peer – or 'lived-experience' – trainers.

I didn't really see this as progress in my recovery and I still didn't expect to get a lot better. I certainly wasn't confident that I'd had my last hospital admission. What I remember thinking strongly was that I could help others with their recovery, or at the very least equip the mentally ill and the health professionals who attended courses with greater understanding of severe mental illness.

As it happened, later in 2017 I was to undergo a series of electroconvulsive therapy (ECT) treatments for the first time. The outcome was that I have splintered memories of both the Train the Trainer course and my subsequent involvement with training, but I will do my best to recount what I can.

I definitely remember finding the Train the Trainer team inspiring, understanding, compassionate and fun. As with all recovery college courses, both those with lived and learned experience of mental illness were involved. I enjoyed preparing and delivering mini presentations each day and getting feedback, as well as offering feedback to other students on the course.

Because of ongoing issues with my mental health, I never became an accredited trainer, but completing the practical components of the course led to an invitation to get involved in co-producing and co-delivering a new course called 'Understanding Psychosis'.

Again, it's difficult to write about this because I only have fragments of memory in relation to the whole process, but I can say with certainty that I threw myself into it, truly believing that I was contributing to something worthwhile. I enjoyed working on an equal footing with the psychiatrist who provided the learned experience, and was delighted when student feedback on the course was overwhelmingly positive.

I remember having a chat with the co-ordinator of the college afterwards and going home with an application form to formalise my volunteering in co-production. This was in the summer of 2017.

That form was never submitted. Within days of the last session of Understanding Psychosis, my own psychosis engulfed me. I ended up being readmitted to hospital yet again.

I had no idea that it would be four years before I took another recovery college course. However, an important seed had been planted. I had met a group of people who believed that recovery was possible for everyone. I didn't yet share that belief, but when I came to revisit the concept later, it was not with complete ignorance. The foundations for my own recovery journey had been laid.

What is recovery-focused mental healthcare?

Until the mid-1970s, most mental health professionals believed that people with serious mental illness (schizophrenia, bipolar disorder and schizoaffective disorder) would be chronically unwell and unable to function in society, primarily residing in institutions.[2] Around this time, two trends emerged: first, studies began to show that people with these conditions were able to live satisfying lives in the community with the right support; and second, people with serious mental illness began to realise for themselves that they could live within the community and share their stories.

Disability rights activists took up the cause of people with serious mental illness and began to advocate for them to be included in decisions about their care. This created what has become known as the 'recovery movement', though this was very much a minority concern, led by sufferers rather than professionals, until the 1990s. It was only in 2003 (in the US) and 2009 (in the UK) that recovery-focused care became enshrined in mental health policy.[3]

How is recovery defined in this context?

Most definitions of recovery in recovery-focused mental healthcare make it clear that it does not equate to 'cure'. However, it describes a series of very positive life-changes . . .

In the USA, mental health policy is promoted by the Substance Abuse and Mental Health Services Administration (SAMHSA), which, in 2006, defined recovery as 'a journey of healing and transformation enabling a person with a mental health problem to live a meaningful life in a community of his or her choice while striving to achieve his or her full potential'.[4] In 2011, their revised definition suggested that recovery is 'a process of change through which individuals improve their health and wellness, live a self-directed life, and strive to reach their full potential'.[5]

In both the US and the UK, a distinction is often made between traditional 'clinical recovery' and 'personal recovery' (as promoted by the recovery movement), for which the most commonly used definition was coined by William Anthony: 'A deeply personal, unique process of changing one's attitudes, values, feelings, goals, skills, and/or roles. It is a way of living a satisfying, hopeful, and contributing life even within the limitations caused by illness. Recovery involves the development of new meaning and purpose in one's life as one grows beyond the catastrophic effects of mental illness.'[6]

Ten guiding principles
In 2012, SAMHSA outlined ten fundamental principles of recovery-focused care, which I have summarised here:[7]

1. Hope: The message of recovery is that the future can be better, and barriers can be overcome.
2. Peer support: Sharing of experiential knowledge and skills.
3. Individualised and person-centred: Based on a person's experience, needs and preferences.
4. Strengths: Building on individuals' resiliencies, talents and coping abilities.
5. Respect: For consumers, including protecting their rights and ending stigma.
6. Holistic: Reflecting mental, physical, emotional, spiritual and community health needs.
7. Responsibility: Of consumers for their self-care and recovery journeys.
8. Self-direction: Consumer-led and controlled care.
9. Non-linear: Allowing for setbacks and learning by experience.
10. Empowerment: Consumers educated and supported in making decisions about their care.

I believe that these ten principles are indeed fundamental to personal recovery, and I have linked one or two to each chapter in this book.

Where do healthcare systems stand in relation to such a recovery model today?

According to the American Psychological Association, a recovery-focused framework is 'one which is driven by the person with the illness and one which operates from a belief, shared by the mental health team, and actively communicated to the person, that recovery can occur and should be expected'.[8]

They acknowledge that this still does not always occur in the US because professionals are unaware of interventions that help, because they may not see the economic benefits of allocating resources to recovery-focused therapy and because they are reluctant to abandon the traditional focus on medication and psychotherapy.

In my experience, health professionals in the UK are now beginning to acknowledge recovery-focused care. This is led in each health trust by recovery colleges, but is not always consistent across primary systems of mental healthcare.

Stephanie Bennett, a peer trainer and former peer support worker

Stephanie is a mum and a Christian with lived experience of mental ill health. She works as a peer trainer at a recovery college in Northern Ireland.

What does a peer support worker do within the college?

It's really about being a point of contact. Students coming to the college for the first time are often anxious. I am there to link in with them before they come along; to reassure them that this is a safe place to come. I might arrange to meet them at the door when they arrive, or to give them a phone call on the morning that they are due to come. As peer support workers at the recovery college, we all had a first day, we all attended courses ourselves before taking on this role, so we can tell them that we really do understand how anxious they may feel.

It's a case of sharing from my lived experience in a hopeful way. If it's appropriate, I might say that at one time I was really unwell – that I spent time in hospital – but the more important thing is sharing about my recovery and how I've developed strategies for living that work for me. It's a journey, and all of us peer support workers still have our difficult days, but life is definitely so much better than it was. The most important thing, I think, is that we offer *realistic*, rather than *idealistic*, hope. I think when new students are anxious and I share my journey, they start to think, 'Well, the recovery college must be okay if you felt that way too and now you work here!'

I also offer further support. For example, I might go to a course with a student, either because they just need that emotional support or if they have another particular need. I recently went along to a course with a student who was visually impaired as well as having mental ill health, who needed practical help with his course.

Do you think peer support workers are valued members of the recovery college team?

Absolutely! Peer support is at the heart of what the recovery college does. It is a core value. Our recovery college slogan is 'Hope, control and opportunity', and those are real values. We peer support workers embody those values. In fact, all the peer support workers and peer trainers who work for the college have had mental ill health, so it's a very supportive environment. The culture is one of checking in with one another, and there's a big focus on self-care. The professionals who come in to do co-production and co-delivery respect our roles as well.

You are a Christian. Is faith valued within the recovery college?

I think in the recovery-focused model of mental healthcare, people are very open to the idea of faith and spirituality, and tend to be less judgemental and dismissive of faith than people might be in more traditional mental healthcare services. They really acknowledge that if something helps someone to move forward in their recovery, including a Christian faith, then that is to be valued.

For example, they might talk about meds being an option for dealing with a crisis, but also mention that some people find prayer helpful – whereas I think in some healthcare settings people are scared to mention things like prayer. I can certainly go to a course and say, as a peer, 'My faith is important to me and brings me hope.'

When I talked about your book, *Wrestling with My Thoughts*, staff within the college were keen to read about your journey, even though Christian faith was a big part of it. Of course, faith in Northern Ireland is a complicated issue with political association. I think maybe in recovery colleges elsewhere in the UK it might be even easier to talk about faith issues. Most colleges, including ourselves, run a course on 'Spirituality for Recovery', which is generic spirituality, but it's acknowledged that this spirituality might come from a Christian faith.

Dr Ken Yeow, a consultant psychiatrist

Dr Yeow works within the NHS and has experience in General Adult Psychiatry, Eating Disorders and Learning Disability. He is a Christian and the author of *Personal Freedom: How the gospel can be good for your mental health.*

Who can recover from mental illness?

I think the response to this question hinges on which definition of 'recover' is being used.

If 'recover' is taken to mean a complete amelioration of symptoms, a reversal of underlying causative pathology and a full return to premorbid levels of functioning, it would be unrealistic to expect that everyone will recover. This would pertain to mental illnesses that have a clear association with abnormal brain structure and function, e.g., dementia, neurodevelopmental disorders, certain psychotic illnesses, some severe mood disorders, mental health conditions related to chronic physical disease, etc.

If 'recover' is taken to mean the potential for effective resolution in terms of more minor, less biological-based conditions and the possibility of optimisation of quality of life where there is more serious illness, then this could be a more universal expectation. It is always the intention of mental health professionals to try to treat and support their patients to achieve as much improvement as they can, even in situations where the longer-term prognosis may be less favourable.

A key aim is to try to help someone with a mental illness to hold on to hope. Distressing symptoms may be able to be improved even if underlying illness is not curable. Anyone with a mental illness should be helped to feel that they have intrinsic value and can contribute positively to this world. There are many sufferers who go on to be effectual helpers of others because of the understanding and empathy borne out of their own journey. For some, just keeping going is itself a huge achievement.

Scripture and reflection

The CHIME factors

In 2011, Mary Leamy and her UK-based research group realised there had been many studies about personal recovery, but no real consensus about what needed to happen for this recovery to occur. They examined ninety-seven studies to work out what they had in common and identified five recovery processes.[9]

These processes were: connectedness, hope, identity, meaning and empowerment, from which they came up with the acronym 'CHIME'. Since 2011, professionals using the recovery model have been able to use these CHIME factors to assess whether someone is moving forward in recovery.

I find the CHIME factors interesting because I can see how important they are to people of all faiths and none, but also how a Christian faith makes each one so much more potent.

Connectedness

I am the vine; you are the branches. If you remain in me and I in you, you will bear much fruit; apart from me you can do nothing.
(John 15:5)
Now you are the body of Christ, and each one of you is a part of it.
(1 Corinthians 12:27)

Recovery practitioners talk about the importance of peer support; connections with family, friends and neighbours; feeling connected to a place and community; and having supportive connections with healthcare professionals. As a Christian on a recovery journey, I have additional connections: to Christ and to his people, the Church.

In John 15, Jesus tells his followers they are connected to him as branches to a vine. In verse 16 he goes on to say that he chose them and has appointed them to bear fruit that will last. My recovery is all the more secure and lasting because I remain in him.

In his first letter to the Corinthians, Paul writes that the Church represents the body of Christ, each part having a role, and each part needing the other if the body is to function (12:21, 27). As a Christian, I am connected to others in the Church; I am a vital member with a function; I need others, and they need me.

Having connectedness with Christ and with the Church is a great advantage in recovery, but those other connections – with peers, health professionals and wider society – are also to be valued. Just because I am a Christian does not mean that I should not avail myself of common grace supports within my community. Connectedness here also gives me opportunities to share my faith (see John 17:18).

Hope

We have this hope as an anchor for the soul, firm and secure.
(Hebrews 6:19)

The LORD is good to those whose hope is in him, to the one who seeks him.
(Lamentations 3:25)

Recovery practitioners aim to inspire hope through believing for their clients that positive change is possible, and peer support can generate hope through the sharing of 'recovery stories'. Yet this kind of hope, by definition, suggests that there is no *certainty* of recovery.

As a Christian, I have biblical hope, which is defined quite differently. John Piper wrote: 'Hope is faith in the future tense. So most of faith is hope.'[10] And, as we are told in Hebrews 11:1: 'Now faith is confidence in what we hope for and assurance about what we do not see.' I can have confidence; I can have assurance.

I have a certain and biblical hope. Hope that originates from God is so much more powerful and motivating in my recovery than any hope generated by health professionals or peers. (In the final chapter of this book, I write of my certain hope of recovery beyond this world. You might choose to read that now or at any point in your journey where you feel worn down in this life.)

Identity

Identity is a huge issue in modern society. Many of us find identity in our sexuality, race or occupation. We may lose our identity at the end of a relationship or with redundancy. Struggling with identity is a rite of passage for today's young people.

So God created mankind in his own image,
    in the image of God he created them;
    male and female he created them.
(Genesis 1:27)

See what great love the Father has lavished on us, that we should be called children of God! And that is what we are!
(1 John 3:1)

Therefore, there is now no condemnation for those who are in Christ Jesus.
(Romans 8:1)

But you are a chosen people, a royal priesthood, a holy nation, God's special possession.
(1 Peter 2:9)

As a Christian, I have found peace in embracing the identity given to me by God, even though living as me has not always been peaceful.

When people are first diagnosed with severe mental illness, it often seems to become their identity. I remember a time when the first thing that tripped off my tongue after I introduced myself was, '. . . and I have schizoaffective disorder.'

In the recovery model, the idea is to gently shift the focus so that the diagnosis is less central. Psychologist, research scientist and survivor of schizophrenia, Dr Pat Deegan developed a famous illustration showing a person's identity as a flower, in which the mental illness starts out as the centre of the flower but later becomes only one of many petals.[11] So in my case, for example, there might also be petals representing my roles as mother, wife, daughter, writer, musician, lover of the outdoors, and so on.

This is clearly an important shift, but as a Christian, the central part of the flower is the key to my identity and found there are three key facts: I am created in the image of God; I am one of God's children; and I am in Christ Jesus. I could go on to add many other descriptions: that I am chosen, that I am a priest, that I am holy . . .

Thus, as a Christian, I have the strongest possible sense of identity beyond my illness as a foundation for my recovery.

Meaning (and purpose)

Therefore go and make disciples of all nations, baptising them in the name of the Father and of the Son and of the Holy Spirit, and teaching them to obey everything I have commanded you.
(Matthew 28:19–20)

> For we are God's handiwork, created in Christ Jesus to do good
> works, which God prepared in advance for us to do.
> (Ephesians 2:10)

> But you will receive power when the Holy Spirit comes on you; and
> you will be my witnesses in Jerusalem, and in all Judea and Samaria,
> and to the ends of the earth.
> (Acts 1:8)

Mary Leamy and her colleagues identified that people who find meaning
and purpose in life do better in recovery, whether through family and
relationships; work, education or creative pursuits; making sense of
their mental illness; or spirituality.

Setting my faith (my spirituality) aside, it can be hard to feel as though
life has much meaning. If we really were tiny products of evolutionary
processes living on a planet that is just a speck of dust in the universe, it
would be easy to conclude, with the writer of Ecclesiastes: 'Everything
is meaningless!' (12:8).

Instead, as a Christian, I understand the true arc of history: how
God created humankind for relationship with him and entered into
successive covenants with us – including the new covenant sealed
through Jesus' incarnation, death and resurrection. I can find meaning in
the fact that I was created to worship him (Isaiah 43:21).

Aside from meaning and purpose, which I can and do find
through family and work, I have a higher purpose, clearly defined
for me in the New Testament. I am called to make disciples of all
nations, and I was created to do good works prepared in advance
by God.

But the beginnings of meaning and purpose can be found in small
things. As we see in Acts 1:8, Jesus *first* sent his disciples to Jerusalem,
then to Judea and Samaria, and *then* to the ends of the earth. I first find
meaning in my immediate environs, and my 'good works' are a witness
to my friends and community.

Empowerment

> The LORD Almighty is with us;
> the God of Jacob is our fortress.
> (Psalm 46:7)

The three key aspects of empowerment identified in the ninety-seven studies about recovery were personal responsibility, control over life and focusing on strengths.

As a Christian, I believe that I am justified 'through faith' (Romans 5:1), but the need to take personal responsibility is taught throughout Scripture, for example in Proverbs 28:13: 'Whoever conceals their sins does not prosper, but the one who confesses and renounces them finds mercy.'

I can have a level of control over my life, but I can be further empowered by handing control over to God; not to abdicate responsibility for decision-making, but to allow myself to be led by the one who is all-seeing and all-knowing.

I can work on my strengths and see these as spiritual gifts (Romans 12:6–8), but I can also know that God's inexhaustible power – too great to be defined – is made perfect in my weakness (2 Corinthians 12:9). He knows my every need (Philippians 4:19).

An awareness of God's power at work in my life is itself empowering and helpful to my recovery.

Questions for personal reflection or discussion

1. How does it make you feel to read that 'recovery' is not the same as 'cure'?
2. As Christians, how can we harness the CHIME factors to help others in their recovery journeys?

2
Sun and rain

Medication and talking therapy

'Plans fail for lack of counsel, but with many advisors they succeed.'
(Proverbs 15:22)

Recovery principle 3
'Culture and cultural background in all of its diverse representations – including values, traditions, and beliefs – are keys in determining a person's journey and unique pathway to recovery.'

'You get to the end of your treatment and your services, and you have virtually no symptoms but you're just sitting there doing nothing, there's nothing else in your life – that's not recovery. That's maybe stability or maybe safety, but that's existing, not actually living.'[1]
(Mark Ragins MD, psychiatrist and medical director, Mental Health America Los Angeles)

Clutching at straws

'I have seen all the things that are done under the sun; all of them are meaningless, a chasing after the wind.'
(Ecclesiastes 1:14)

For me, 2017 and 2018 were years of clutching at straws. I was stuck in a revolving door of hospital admissions and discharges, and every time I went home I had another bright plan for a fresh new start in life.

My first idea was to pursue a career in skincare, which led me to enrol on a practical beauty therapy course at my local further education college and a distance-learning course in dermatological treatments.

My rationale was that it would lead to a people-oriented, hands-on kind of job, practised in a clinic, and therefore having similarities to my original chosen career as a doctor. I'd developed an interest in skincare because my own skin had deteriorated so badly from some of my mental health drugs, and I'd seen how an improvement in this could boost confidence – not to mention how, on the worst days, some carefully applied makeup could have the same effect.

I lasted a couple of months, and the teachers on the practical course could not have been more encouraging. 'You have just the right kind of touch,' they said as I gave a hand massage, 'firm, yet gentle.' A doctor had once said the same thing as I examined a patient's abdomen. I felt hopeful. Perhaps this was my route to a more normal life.

Sadly, psychosis struck again. I was taking a sedative anti-psychotic at the time, and I remember that, after the dose was increased, I once began to snore on the plinth while another student was using me as a model to demonstrate a facial treatment. Embarrassed, I explained the situation to my tutor, who said that she already knew I was unwell . . . my eyes were 'dead'.

I was readmitted to hospital shortly after this, and had soon missed too much of the practical course to rejoin it. I began to question my motives for starting it, in any case. *Do I really want to be a beautician?* I asked myself. *Is it part of God's plan for me?* I didn't feel sure.

When I was next discharged, I took up a proofreading course by correspondence. Though very different, again it seemed a rational thing to do. I liked to read, there was meant to be plenty of this kind of work available, and it was something that would be flexible, that I could do at home in the hours when I felt most well.

My first assignments received high marks and my tutor told me I was a most promising student. A month or two later, he responded to my submissions with 'some disappointment'. I was making frequent mistakes, missing important errors. My mental health had again deteriorated, and I had realised that proofreading is not like reading at all. It takes tremendous focus; something I couldn't muster much of when battling psychotic depression.

Following the next hospital admission, I stumbled upon freelance work editing medical papers by researchers for whom English was a second language. It was interesting, and I was actually making money, but the same situation replayed itself. I started to make mistakes and my rate of pay was reduced accordingly. As my mental health failed, I could not meet my deadlines. I had to give up.

Even though I continued to move in and out of hospital as 2018 went on, I began to have a clearer sense of God at work in my life. I was writing a lot about faith and my mental illness, with the thought that some of my copy might one day be published.

I was also becoming convinced of the need to go deeper in my understanding of the Bible, and a subtle shift occurred in my thinking. With skincare, proofreading or editing, I was looking for something vocational that would become a route to a 'valid' job (in the eyes of others). Now I began to see that study could have value in itself, even if it never led to work . . . even if I stayed unwell.

In the September of 2018, I excitedly enrolled on a graduate diploma course in Theology, a kind of conversion course for people who already had a primary degree in another subject but wanted an equivalent qualification to a BA in Theology. On my first day, as I scribbled on my lecture handouts and spent time in the library, I had a strong sense that I had relinquished my striving and come home.

In that same month, I received a phone call that told me I had been offered a contract to write *Wrestling with My Thoughts*. I knew then that I was going to be a Christian writer. I felt as though my heart would burst. Life suddenly felt promising and worthwhile.

But even this could not keep me well. Fearful of losing a hefty tuition fee, I hastily withdrew from my Theology course three weeks later, as again I was overwhelmed by depression and the prodrome of psychosis to which I had become so accustomed. I remember this feeling a hundred times more disappointing than having to give up proofreading or medical editing, and several times more difficult than giving up on skincare, which I had at least enjoyed.

I was soon back in hospital yet again, though this time I had a laptop with me – ready to work on my book.

Firefighting

What was the medical team doing for me during all these admissions? Why did I never seem to gain any stability? First, even aside from the chronic nature of my illness, it was not entirely their fault that I ended up being readmitted so quickly on so many occasions. The system within which they worked did not facilitate good continuity of care, as the inpatient and home teams had different leaders and different priorities, and communication between the two was not always optimal. Second, I must take part-responsibility myself.

The admissions typically followed a pattern. Admitted in crisis, I would spend a few days wandering about in a fog, often pacing the corridors until it was time for another dose of a tranquillising drug. I would beat myself up emotionally: *Why couldn't you cope at home? Why do you keep letting this happen?* And with every admission I felt more and more hopeless, until I eventually resigned myself to the idea that, with the kind of diagnosis I had, this was what the rest of my life would look like.

As I acclimatised to ward life, the nursing staff would monitor my mental state. They took note of my behaviour and spent time talking with me each day, so they could assess my mood and the content of my thoughts. Within the first week I would be reviewed by the consultant psychiatrist, who primarily based his early decisions on reports from the nursing staff.

This usually happened during a ward round or multidisciplinary team meeting, which would take place weekly in a small room just off the main communal area. I was always brought in towards the end of the meeting to hear the team's plan and offer any views I had, and I don't think I once attended without a cup of tea in one hand and a soggy tissue in the other. I was always in tears.

And each time the doctor would acknowledge my sense of being back for 'yet another admission', with a comment to the effect that it was nice to see me again, even if the circumstances were unfortunate.

I was usually desperate for some big change in treatment strategy – a change in meds or at least in dosage – but, aside from allowing for extra 'PRN' (*pro re nata* or 'as-needed') medication, the team would usually advise waiting a bit longer before instituting any changes. That way, they could get a sense of how I really was and what the best course of action might be.

Inevitably, though, by week two or three we would begin to discuss some new drug to try, or the option of another course of ECT. These decisions weren't taken willy-nilly, though sometimes it felt as though we were taking a shot in the dark. I was always involved; the psychiatrist always considered the possible risks and benefits, interactions with other drugs I was taking and side effects; and there was always a plan for monitoring and a 'Plan B' should the change prove unsuccessful.

I remember one occasion in 2018 when, at the suggestion of my consultant, Dr Francis, I carefully listed every psychotropic drug I had ever taken, along with why it was stopped, my own perception of its effectiveness and any side effects I remembered. This led to him identifying my current antipsychotic medication as the most likely to work and the least likely to cause unwanted problems. A worthwhile exercise indeed.

But I was often impatient to see change, and had to be reminded again and again by nurses that most psychiatric drugs need to be worked up slowly to a therapeutic dose, and that even then it can take time for the body and mind to respond. ECT worked more quickly, but I found it teasing. I would feel better for a day or two after each treatment, then find myself back at square one.

Whether it was a new antipsychotic, a different antidepressant or a change in dose of mood stabiliser, there was usually an effect within a month or so. By this stage I would have settled into the routine of the ward, with its tea breaks and occupational therapy sessions, and time spent exercising, in the quiet room or in the garden. In the early weeks the rhythms were soothing; later they would become tedious.

The problem with me was that every time I began to feel a little better, every time I felt a smile creep across my face, every time I got through a few hours without crying, I found myself desperately wanting to go home. I didn't see the point of staying in hospital any longer than I absolutely had to. As I saw it, my life was to be punctuated by hospital stays anyway, so I might as well spend any good days, when I felt reasonably well, at home with Rob.

Time after time I gathered myself, brushed my hair and asked if I could *please* be transferred to the care of the Home Treatment Team. I often pressurised the nurses into having a doctor assess me for discharge the very same day! Time after time the ward team would try to persuade me that I was being too hasty, to give things a bit longer, but I would push back until I convinced them I could cope at home.

Looking back, it's easy to feel frustrated with myself for being too impulsive and short-sighted. How many times did a discharge have to fail before I realised that rushing home at the first sign of improvement was not effective behaviour?

It's equally easy to feel frustrated with the doctors, who seemed to collude in this firefighting approach – discharging me home until the next inevitable crisis. But they may have felt they had no choice. I was not a risk to myself or anyone else, so they couldn't detain me. And I always had a plausible story: I was going to study beauty or proofreading or theology . . . Whatever the new focus, it would surely bring some stability.

This has *got* to stop!

The following year, 2019, began in much the same vein. At home for Christmas and New Year, my mood began to plummet, and I stumbled into another crisis at the beginning of February. I was admitted, and this time the psychiatrist began to talk about starting regular outpatient ECT to see if that would keep me well enough to avoid such frequent admissions.

I was intrigued by the idea, but somewhat reluctant by this stage, because it was becoming apparent that I had lost segments of memory following the two previous series of ECT. Before any firm plans were made, my mood seemed to lift a bit and, true to form, I asked to be transferred back to the Home Treatment Team.

There followed a two-week period in which I deteriorated very rapidly. My February admission had been due to depression, and my thinking had remained rational and clear. At home I became deluded, believing I was the victim of a conspiracy on a cosmic scale. The 'evil presence' and 'tormentors' returned, and I was convinced the mental health nurses who were trying to help me could not be trusted. I ended up being readmitted.

Only this time, under a different psychiatrist . . .

* * *

A sudden draught catches my bare ankles beneath the table. I cross them and shiver. The double doors to the garden swing closed again.

I sit alone, facing towards the nurses' station; huddled over the table, gripping my mug of tea with both hands. My fingers are trembling. The hot liquid ripples.

Figures cast their shadows over me, but I keep my eyes focused slightly ahead and downwards. In my peripheral vision, the tormentors flap their shadowy wings. I exist in a maelstrom of greys and blacks. I squeeze my eyes tight shut, then slowly open them again.

Hard-soled shoes click across the floor, stopping just to my right. A thin hand leans on my table, but I don't look up.

'May I?'

A tall man has pulled out the chair beside me. I shudder. He sits down, but gives me space.

'Sharon, my name is Dr Ivanov. I will be the psychiatrist working with you on this admission. I wondered if you would be willing to speak with me.'

I shake my head, hunch my shoulders closer to my ears.

He tries again. 'I understand that you are feeling afraid, but I think that I can perhaps help if you would just be willing to give me a few moments.'

Something about his tone, or perhaps even his accent, generates enough curiosity that I look up for just a second and catch a kind eye.

'Sharon?'

I edge my chair back a little, turning away from him as I zip up my cardigan. Then, head dipped, I stand up. He gestures towards an open interview room, and I begin to walk towards it. He follows me.

'Do sit down.'

'I can't talk to you.' My voice sounds too loud.

'That is okay. I know you are feeling very unsafe, but I believe you are safe here. And I know that I only want to help you. Would you like to tell me as much as you feel comfortable with about what you are feeling?'

'It's not safe. I . . . I can't trust anyone. I don't trust anyone. I don't want to talk to anyone.'

'Thank you for explaining that. I do not need you to talk more than you want to.'

I feel a little tension easing in my shoulders. I take a sip of tea, run a hand through my hair.

'Sharon, I think the reason you feel this way is that you are unwell. I think, as you have done before, that you are suffering from psychosis. You are on haloperidol [an antipsychotic], and if you are agreeable, I would like to increase it a little, just for a few days, to see if you feel any improvement.'

It doesn't feel to me like psychosis; I just know I'm not safe here. But his voice is soothing, and he speaks almost with deference. I find myself nodding.

'You agree? Just to try this? I will meet with you again after two days, and you can tell me how you feel.'

There is a moment of eye contact. He wears thin-rimmed glasses, and his features are serious, inquisitive, gentle.

Partly because I want to escape, partly because I want to believe that this unusual man can help me, I assent.

'Okay, so we will try 2.5 mg twice a day instead of 1.5 mg.' He scribbles in my chart. 'I have put you down for an extra 1 mg dose now as a stat, just so we can start as if from this morning.'

I nod.

'Thank you for talking with me, Sharon. Let me walk you to the nurses' room and we will find someone to give you that medication.'

He holds the door open for me and I shuffle out.

* * *

Dr Ivanov did meet with me again after the weekend, by which time I had settled on the higher dose of haloperidol and was less convinced that the healthcare team was plotting against me. I had been able to sleep and was beginning to interact a little with other patients.

A week later, I was sitting quietly in my room one day when a firm knock at the door startled me. When I opened it, Dr Ivanov was standing there with a clipboard and my notes. He asked if I was free to speak with him and took me to a small, rarely used piano room with a view out to the garden.

The first thing he said was, 'This has got to stop! Fifteen admissions in the past three years? We have to break this cycle!'

I remember thinking that no one had ever suggested to me that the cycle *could* stop. We had only ever talked in terms of getting me to feel a bit calmer, a bit less tearful or able to tolerate my pain a bit more. We had dealt with life in terms of having a better day or a better week, but never in terms of securing a better future.

I had come to a point of acceptance that I would probably spend as much as half my time as an inpatient for the foreseeable future. I was very ill, and I had grown quite accustomed to it.

A new direction

Yet this new doctor didn't see it that way. He wanted change, and he was prepared to invest time and energy to bring it about. For the next few weeks he spent a lot of time with me, going over the medications and therapies I had taken (much as Dr Francis had done), and exploring the exact nature of my symptoms and how I experienced them.

We talked about the very physical way in which I experienced depression in my body; the way it felt like an illness causing me to be heavy and achy and slow and exhausted; how sometimes I couldn't tell just from my thoughts and emotions that I was depressed; how a sick feeling in my throat was often the first indicator that something was wrong.

We talked about the nature of the psychosis from which I was gradually emerging, and tried to work out whether it was primary or secondary to my depression on this occasion.

We talked about the remaining positives in my life: relationships with Rob and other friends and family members; faith; enjoyment of yoga and running; my writing (including *Wrestling with My Thoughts*, which was at copy-editing stage and almost ready for publication) and my pets.

I didn't realise it at the time, but these were essentially recovery-focused conversations. We were starting to put the illness 'in its box' and to look at life outside it; forming a picture of what the future might look like if it could be made to become manageable.

Eventually, at a meeting Rob was also involved in, we agreed on a plan. Dr Ivanov had come to feel that, while there had been documented episodes of psychosis in the past when my mood had been fairly normal, recent episodes had occurred in the context of depression, and were probably driven by low mood.

For some years there had been a reluctance on the part of other doctors to prescribe antidepressants for me because I had a history of mania (which can sometimes be triggered by antidepressant use in vulnerable individuals), and that was part of the reason I had been offered ECT instead. Dr Francis had experimented with a tiny, sub-therapeutic dose of a selective serotonin reuptake inhibitor (SSRI) antidepressant, the most prescribed type in the UK, but I had felt agitated while taking it, so it had been stopped.

Dr Ivanov felt I needed long-term treatment for my low mood, and he wasn't convinced the ECT had helped me, so the plan for outpatient ECT was abandoned. Instead, he asked me to consider taking agomelatine, a new antidepressant he believed was unlikely to provoke mania. Nervously, I agreed to try it.

At first I saw little improvement, but a week after the dose had been increased to its maximum I began to feel noticeably better. Previously, I probably would have asked to go home at this point, but somehow I felt differently this time. Dr Ivanov had implanted in me a hope that things really could get better for me if I would just allow him some time to optimise my medication.

A creative approach

Still, he understood that I wanted to be with Rob, and that I had spent a lot of time in hospital, so he began to be creative with the plan for my admission, giving me leave from the ward between 5 pm and 9 pm each day so I could have dinner at home with Rob and a walk together with our dogs.

This went well. A friend who worked near the hospital drove me home each evening, and Rob brought me back in time for my evening medications. The nursing staff monitored me during the day, and I looked forward to several hours in a more normal setting in the evenings.

Dr Ivanov continued to invest time in lengthy conversations with me, forming what I now recognise as a 'longer-term therapeutic alliance', a key feature of recovery-oriented mental healthcare. At the time I just appreciated his willingness to listen, to really hear me, and to respond with wisdom and gentleness, offering just enough of his own life experiences and perspective to make it feel like a two-way relationship.

By 16 July 2019, I had spent four-and-a-half consecutive months in hospital, but I had been on an established drug regimen for some time that I could tolerate comfortably. I was no longer psychotic or depressed, and I had finally come to believe that this might be my last admission. I had successfully spent a lot of time at home without cutting ties with the ward, and hadn't crashed as I often did before.

I also had a discharge plan that made me feel confident. I left the unit with an appointment to begin counselling therapy the following week, and with an offer from a lawyer friend of part-time work as a paralegal – not, I hoped, a chasing-after-the-wind exercise this time, but a genuine opportunity to create some structure and purpose in life, while earning a little money.

The time Dr Ivanov had spent with me was rewarded. Almost five years later, I am still taking the same drugs (with one addition), and I have not once been readmitted. To this day I am thankful for his belief that I could recover and for his tenacity in working with me to break that cycle.

Of course, 16 July was only the beginning. I still had a lot of recovering to do.

A pivotal moment

Where was I spiritually at this point? Throughout this longer admission I had felt close to God and, more so than during previous inpatient stays, had spoken of this with the healthcare team. I spent time almost daily in the quiet room and had weekly visits from ministers at my church.

By this stage I had written, in *Wrestling with My Thoughts*, of three key truths God had revealed to me during my struggles: that he held me, that he is good and that he was giving me strength. At the conclusion of the book, I wrote:

> My journey through severe mental illness has been hard, and I know that I face a future that is likely to involve even more of the same struggles. If that was where the story ended, you would understand if I lived in a state of despair. But I don't. Instead, I rest in the knowledge that I will never fall from God's right hand. He has a proven record of goodness to me

even in times of great pain, and he has upheld his promise to be my strength and my refuge.

I had already come a long way by the time I penned these words – certainly very far from a time in 2008 when I felt utterly abandoned by God and had renounced my faith altogether. By around May 2019 I realised I had reached a pivotal point.

I felt less convinced that I was facing a future 'likely to involve even more of the same struggles', as I had written. I knew there would be struggles, but I had begun to wonder whether they would be different in future. I wrote my first book from a place where I had come to terms with a life marked by severe and chronic illness. Now, allied with a psychiatrist who believed this didn't need to be the case, I began to pray for real change.

Having had to leave the care of Dr Ivanov on discharge from the ward, I formed another important therapeutic alliance when I began to receive counselling. Debbie offered me something I had never had in a counselling relationship before: a commitment to work with me indefinitely, for as long as counselling was useful, rather than for a brief intervention or a limited number of sessions. This kind of willingness to be 'in it for the long haul' with a client is central to recovery-focused care.

I felt that I clicked with Debbie very quickly. The first important shift as I talked with her was that I felt less like 'the patient with schizoaffective disorder in Room 7' and more like 'Sharon, an articulate, independent thinker, who could even be funny at times', as she once described me. I found that it soon became a very validating relationship, where I had previously suffered many invalidating experiences, and that I really appreciated what Debbie had to say.

This regaining of a sense of self beyond the illness is a recognised requirement for personal recovery, as illustrated by Dr Deegan's flower petal model (described in chapter 1), and I don't think I had the wherewithal to do it for myself at this point. I needed Debbie's expert help.

Against a background of feeling validated and accepted as a person, I felt I was getting to know myself again during these sessions, much as an adolescent begins to recognise what sort of person they really are and what they want to be. Debbie gave me the confidence to be a little more assertive in my relationships, rather than so often being submissive, as had seemed appropriate to me when I had viewed myself as mentally incapable.

As Debbie helped me give voice to my true self, I felt empowered. A lot of what we talked about was small stuff – week-to-week decisions that might have seemed inconsequential, but that helped me build towards health and wholeness. I remember that when she decided to read my book (which she deliberately avoided until she felt she knew me for herself), I felt so hugely relieved when she liked it. That affirmation meant so much.

It was also empowering to have some meaningful work during this time of talking therapy. As a part-time paralegal, I was valued and gainfully occupied, building on attributes beyond merely coping with my illness. This positive development helped to expand my horizons and identity.

Debbie shared my Christian faith. I had wanted my long-term counsellor to understand it, as it is so critical to who I am. I had worked with Christian and secular therapists in the past, and had been able to make progress with both, but at this point I felt I needed a spiritual dimension to my therapy. My identity as a follower of Christ was now central; the core of the flower.

Debbie told me later that she set out to create a space where I would feel safe and secure enough to explore my story and the challenges I faced; to be heard, and to develop self-compassion and self-kindness. She definitely succeeded in this. Within the safety of her office, I grew in confidence and self-knowledge over the course of a year, after which we agreed that, for the time being at least, our therapeutic alliance had achieved its goals. By then, my life looked very different.

I cannot stress enough how much professional intervention and engagement were absolutely foundational to my recovery. There was no way that I could have 'pulled myself up by my own bootstraps' from that point in the spring of 2019 when I was depressed and psychotic. My brain chemistry was awry, my thinking was faulty and my mental state was confused.

Medication changes – namely, the antipsychotic started by Dr Francis on a previous admission and increased by Dr Ivanov, and the antidepressant prescribed by Dr Ivanov – were essential to correct the biological component of my illness. Debbie's counselling therapy built on this to help with the emotional and psychosocial aspects of my condition.

Recovery could not have been initiated without these inputs. The length of time I spent in a chronically ill state before these professional interventions is evidence of this! I will be forever grateful for these key individuals. However, it was still early in my recovery journey, with a lot of work left for me to do.

Medication and severe mental illness: a summary

When I left hospital in July 2019, I was taking an antipsychotic drug, an antidepressant and a mood stabiliser. I still take these same drugs today, and as someone with severe and enduring mental illness, I expect that I will probably need them for much, if not all, of my life. But what are these drugs, and how do they work? Here is a very brief summary:

Antipsychotic drugs

Psychosis, the defining feature of severe mental illness, is described as a 'loss of contact with reality'.[2] Many researchers believe that psychotic experiences – and delusions – arise when an excess of dopamine, a neurotransmitter (a chemical that carries messages from one nerve cell to another) is produced in the brain.[3]

Most antipsychotic medications are known to block dopamine receptors, and it is thought that they reduce psychotic experiences by decreasing the flow of dopamine around the brain. They are also involved in altering levels of other brain chemicals, including serotonin and noradrenaline, which may cause them to affect mood.[4]

Antipsychotics are divided into two types: first-generation (or 'typical') antipsychotics, including haloperidol – one of the oldest – which I now take; and second-generation (or 'atypical') antipsychotics. First-generation antipsychotics can cause side effects involving abnormal movements of the muscles. Second-generation antipsychotics are less likely to do this, but have their own side effects, including sedation and weight gain.

Both first- and second-generation antipsychotics have consistently proved effective in treating psychosis. The choice of drug depends on individual patient needs and characteristics.[5] For me, the first antipsychotic that was both tolerable and effective was a first-generation drug, though we found I did need an additional drug to counter its neuromuscular side effects.

Antidepressants

Antidepressant drugs are prescribed to treat depression and a number of other mental health conditions, as well as physical symptoms, such as nerve pain, in some cases. They are very commonly used. In 2017–2018, 17% of the English population received at least one prescription for an antidepressant drug.[6]

There has been some debate over the efficacy of antidepressants in mild depression, but large studies show that they are 20–30% more effective than placebo drugs[7] and are more effective the greater the severity of the depression.[8] So, for depression associated with schizoaffective disorder, which I have, it was very likely that an antidepressant would help. The challenge was to find one I could tolerate.

Antidepressants lift mood by boosting or prolonging the activity of specific neurotransmitters.[9] Most work on the serotonin or noradrenaline systems, but agomelatine, the one I take now, primarily works by increasing melatonin activity.[10] It is not possible to demonstrate a chemical imbalance in the brain and then correct it with antidepressants; we just know that they alter brain chemistry and that this often helps.[11]

Mood stabilisers

I take mood stabilisers, lithium and lamotrigine, because I have had episodes of depression and mania (my schizoaffective disorder is of a bipolar type). They are also licensed for bipolar disorder and severe, recurrent depression.[12]

When we talk of mood stabilisers, the drugs concerned are variable in structure and action, but all work to bring balance and stability to mood. Lithium, anti-seizure medications and some antipsychotics may all be prescribed for this purpose, and many have proven to be effective.[13]

A note about naming drugs

Before writing this book, I had a policy of not naming the medications I take (or have tried) in my writing or public speaking. The reason for this is that psychiatric medications tend to affect different people very differently. I didn't want to create the impression that my drugs are the best or to encourage people to ask for these medications, which have been effective for me, when they might not be as effective for them.

To avoid being overly vague in this book, I have chosen to name my medications. Those that I now take have been pivotal to my journey and foundational to my recovery. Please let me reiterate that others may have different brain chemistry, experience different side effects, or for other reasons find my medications unsuitable. That does not mean that they may not be worthwhile options to discuss with healthcare providers in the context of similarly severe mental illness.

The UK organisation Mind provides 'advice and support to empower anyone experiencing a mental health problem'. It has an informative website, which includes helpful descriptions of different psychiatric medications (www.mind.org.uk/information-support/drugs-and-treatments).

Gordon McConville

Gordon McConville is Professor Emeritus of Old Testament Theology at the University of Gloucestershire, having also taught at Trinity College in Bristol and Wycliffe Hall in Oxford. He has published many articles and books on aspects of the Old Testament, and has a particular interest in its use in Christian theology and contemporary application. Gordon is also my uncle.

What does the Old Testament say about recovery?

The prophet Jeremiah laments: 'Is there no balm in Gilead; is there no healer there? Why then has the health of the daughter of my people not recovered?' (Jeremiah 8:22, Gordon's own translation).

The rhetorical question here is poignant, because it rests on the premise that there is indeed a healer in Gilead (meaning in Israel). The metaphor of 'healer' is applied frequently to God in the Old Testament, and expresses his fundamental disposition towards his people. The psalmist knows that he 'heals the broken-hearted' (Psalm 107:20). Hosea, in a moving passage, depicts God as a parent, taking up his children (Israel), and, in love and compassion, healing them (Hosea 11:3–4).

God's healing is applied to the whole human person, so it embraces physical and mental health. He 'heals all your diseases' (Psalm 103:3 – a psalm addressed by the psalmist to himself, or to his 'soul'). But it is also addressed to the whole human condition, including the moral and spiritual dimensions. For this reason, healing is often paired with being saved (Jeremiah 17:14) and forgiven (Psalm 103:3). This does not imply a direct link between sin and illness, a notion that is firmly rejected in the Old Testament (for example in Job; Psalm 73; Isaiah 53). Rather, illness is enmeshed in the griefs of a fallen world.

The Old Testament tells the underlying story of God's will to heal this unperfected world. It surfaces in many indicative ways: when Elijah and Elisha raise children from the dead and restore them to their impoverished mothers (1 Kings 17:17–24; 2 Kings 4:8–37); in the healing of King Hezekiah to continue his beneficent rule in Judah (2 Kings 20:1–11); in Ezekiel's famous vision of resurrection in the valley of dry bones (Ezekiel 37:1–14); in the promise of death swallowed up 'for ever' (Isaiah 25:8). All of these are components in the great narrative of God's purpose to redeem his broken world.

We live in a 'meantime', in the actuality of the broken world that still awaits perfecting. Our diseases, and death itself, are part of this picture.

How then might we think of recovery? The answer lies deeper than the individual recoveries that may come to us by God's grace along the way. It consists rather in the practice of faithful hope that God is renewing all things. Such hope is cultivated (by the psalmists) in the regularities of communal worship, the nurturing of memories of God's past goodness, the purposeful address to one's soul in the manner of Psalm 103, using the language of faith the Scriptures have given us. Recovery is living in the knowledge and hope of God's willingness to heal, and the patience to persevere and wait.

Scripture and reflection

Spiritual – and medical – milk

'Like newborn babies, crave pure spiritual milk, so that by it you may grow up in your salvation, now that you have tasted that the Lord is good' (1 Peter 2:2–3).

My little son is nineteen months old and a picky eater, but he does consume a certain range of foods. It seems like no time since he was a newborn, and back then he was what some might call a 'guzzler'. He could down a bottle of formula milk – his first food – in minutes!

At that time, my son was not ready for solids. For the first few months of life, all he needed was one whole food: milk. But this milk enabled him to grow and develop, so that, in time, he could begin to take baby rice, then pureed fruit and vegetables, and ultimately the textured foods he eats today.

When the apostle Peter wrote to the Christians in Asia Minor, they were undergoing persecution at the hands of the Roman emperor, Nero. Thus, the themes of Peter's letter were holiness in a hostile environment and hope during suffering.[14]

These new Christians, probably Jews and Gentiles, had tasted that the Lord was good (or, in some translations, 'kind')[15], and Peter encouraged them to crave more of this 'spiritual milk' (2:2), so they could 'grow up in their salvation' . . . living holy, hope-filled lives in a difficult context.

Early in my recovery journey, my psychological environment was hostile, and I had persecutory delusions. I, too, needed basic food for growth. This came through medications that altered the chemical environment bathing my brain. In a sense, these drugs were my 'medical milk'. Once I had committed to an effective medication regimen, I could begin my real growth in recovery.

And of course, Peter's spiritual message applied to me too. In my difficult context, I needed to drink spiritual milk, the milk of God's kindness and goodness, presented to me through the gospel, so I could 'grow up in my salvation' even as I grew in my recovery.

Spiritual milk and medical milk together nourished me on my journey towards wholeness. Like the Christians in Asia Minor, I want to live a holy life. I also need hope in times of suffering. Like my baby son, my diet is no longer limited to milk, but I needed to 'guzzle' it in those early days, and must continue to drink it to ensure complete nutrition.

Look at any newborn baby handed to his mother, and you will see him migrate instinctively to her breast. My prayer is that we Christians will have the same instinct to seek spiritual milk, looking to God's word, spoken in Scripture, for evidence of his kindness, goodness and love for us.

Questions for personal reflection or discussion

1. What has been your experience of attitudes towards psychiatric drugs among Christians? Have you ever been fed the message that Christians shouldn't take these drugs? If so, has your attitude changed at all after reading this chapter?
2. Do you crave spiritual milk? How do you meet your need for good spiritual nutrition?

3

Germination

Developing a recovery mindset

'Let us run with perseverance the race marked out for us.'
(Hebrews 12:1)

Recovery principle 4
'Recovery is built on the multiple capacities, strengths, talents, coping abilities, resources, and inherent value of each individual.'

Recovery principle 5
'Community, systems, and societal acceptance and appreciation for people affected by mental health . . . problems – including protecting their rights and eliminating discrimination – are crucial in achieving recovery.'

'Recovery is not recovery from a disease or condition; recovery is recovery of the person who has the disease or condition.'[1]
(American Psychological Association)

A life-changing discovery

I knew that I was pregnant a week before I took the test. I felt different. I had never been pregnant before, so it wasn't that I recognised the feeling; it just seemed like intuition. I knew that I had become a mother. Over the next few days, physical signs emerged. My breasts looked and felt different, and one day, sitting at my computer in the legal office where I was working, I experienced sudden waves of nausea and dizziness.

So, when the second thin blue line appeared on the urine dipstick, it only confirmed what I already knew. Rob had not experienced the physical symptoms, of course. He thought I was reading the test incorrectly, and when I finally convinced him it was positive, he sent me out to buy another one . . . just to be sure!

Rob and I had talked about our mutual desire to have children long before we were even engaged. In fact, one of the issues that had made him a little unsure about marrying me was a niggling doubt that, given my illness, I might never be able to cope as a parent. In time, we agreed that, if we were to have a child, God would provide sufficient health and the right supports.

But during the cycle of hospital admissions and discharges that began six months after our wedding, both of us knew the timing was not right. Trying for a baby would have been very short-sighted, though we often talked of our hopes that things would change.

I remember asking one of my psychiatrists whether she thought I could ever have a baby. She said that she didn't believe I would ever be a danger to a child, but that I was too unwell to be emotionally available to a little one. It broke my heart because I knew it was true.

My admission under Dr Ivanov altered everything. When I was finally discharged in early July 2019, I was a new person – steady and able to cope with the ups and downs of day-to-day life – something I began to prove early on by sustaining my job as a paralegal. Rob and I had a deep sense that things had changed, that the cycle had been broken. We were filled with hope.

Looking back, it's hard to believe we became so confident so quickly, given the lengthy period in which life had been extremely challenging, but in the early autumn we made an appointment to see our GP. I was thirty-seven, Rob was fifty-nine, and we knew that if we were going to start a family we didn't have a lot of time.

For Dr Smith, the question was simple: 'Do you want a kid?' We did, of course. He also shared our Christian faith and told us that he believed no child was born whom the Lord did not want to have life. His view was that if we had prayed about it and wanted to move forward, we could. He felt that the idea of 'trying for a baby' was a bad one, putting everybody under undue pressure. Instead, we should stop '*not* trying' and let nature take its course.

There were two remaining issues to consider: my medication, and the inevitable concerns of the healthcare team. In terms of medication, I was taking nothing that was considered to be dangerous to an unborn baby (although at least one drug was new and an unknown quantity), but I would definitely not be able to breastfeed.

Dr Smith considered it possible that other professionals might have misgivings. Social workers would want to check that all was well throughout, particularly with regard to psychosis. Some people find that kind of thing intrusive, he said, while others didn't have so much of a problem with it. I remember that we didn't think enough of this at the time to consider it an obstacle.

Rob and I left the consultation encouraged. We talked and prayed more, and in October 2019 we agreed to stop using contraception. Neither of us expected that we would conceive in the first month, but we did.

A recovery-focused psychiatrist

I remember feeling nothing but positive emotions for the first few days after we found out we were pregnant. I was so excited and delighted, and my heart felt as if it would burst! We told my parents, my sister and my aunt, but I found it really difficult not to spill the news to friends as well. Rob was much more measured, and I think a little shocked, but he shared my deep joy.

A week or two on, however, I started to feel anxious about the baby. When I visited Dr Smith to tell him the news, he said that he needed to advise me that around one in five pregnancies ends in miscarriage. From that moment on, if I felt the slightest flush of warmth I thought I was losing my baby. I just couldn't wait for that twelve-week scan to see a tiny heartbeat.

I also started to obsess over minor changes in my moods. Of course, my body was flooded with hormones, and I was also incredibly tired, so it was natural that I would feel a bit different, but I couldn't help thinking about what the previous psychiatrist had said. I wouldn't be emotionally available to a child if I was ill, so I was desperate to be as well as possible.

It was a precarious situation. I was so anxious that everything in the pregnancy would go well that this very anxiety could have affected my mental state more generally and jeopardised my ability to parent. With this in mind, I was eager to have a review with my outpatient psychiatrist, but she had just taken medical retirement and the post was vacant. After a few weeks I was offered a meeting with a locum consultant, Dr King, and I remember making a list of everything I wanted to say to him.

* * *

The TV in the waiting room blares in my left ear. I want to ask the receptionist to switch it off, but another patient sitting opposite me is watching it intently. I plant my feet firmly on the patterned green carpet, trying to control my trembling legs.

'Sharon?'

A young man with a quiff of mousey hair sticks his head through the double doors and makes eye contact with me as I stand up. He gestures for me to follow him.

We enter a small, stuffy but newly refurbished interview room and he seats himself in an office chair at a narrow desk. I sit down in a cushioned chair at an angle to him. The small bin at my feet is overflowing with damp tissues.

He flicks his pen back and forth between his fingers, glancing at my notes as if to remind himself of my name, then introduces himself in an English accent.

'I'm Dr King, Consultant Psychiatrist. I'm new here, but I know the nurses know you well, and I've had a chat with Joanna about you just this morning. I gather congratulations are in order – you're expecting.'

I nod, smiling, but my lower lip quivers a little. 'Thank you.'

'How many weeks now? Seven or so?'

'Eight. My twelve-week scan is next month. I'm so anxious about it.'

'Feeling anxious.' He makes a note. 'That's completely understandable. Do you want to tell me how things are otherwise? You've been doing really well, I hear, and you're working.'

I trip over my words. 'N-n-not any more. I didn't want to travel to Belfast with the sickness and the tiredness, and just – well, I didn't feel I could do it now.' I hear myself sigh. 'My mood's a bit low.'

He makes another note. 'So, you feel you're a bit low, but really I hear you're managing at home and cooking and keeping on top of the housework, and Joanna says you're getting exercise and doing yoga. That's all so great, you know. I think you're doing very well.'

I feel heat creep up the back of my neck. 'I'm worried about being low, with the baby coming. And I can't stop worrying that I'm going to lose my baby. I'm anxious all the time.'

Dr King swivels in his chair and sets down his pen. 'Sharon, I hear you. You're a bit anxious and a bit low. Do you know, that's perfectly normal for this stage in pregnancy? Your hormones are all changing . . . and if you weren't worrying about miscarrying, I'd be surprised – it's natural.'

I keep wanting to interject. But don't you know I've got schizoaffective disorder? But don't you know I've only recently come out of hospital? I need to be well for my baby . . .

He beams at me. I force a smile but feel my face twists instead. I want him to look at my meds, to make a plan, to somehow help me feel that something is going to be done so I can look after my baby in seven months' time.

'Look, I can see you're worried. This is a big life change for you. But really, everything I hear about you is good. I think you are probably mildly depressed and quite anxious, and I think we can help you with that. I'm going to write the name of a book here that I recommend for you. It's a self-help CBT book that's great for the sort of symptoms you're having.' He scribbles almost illegibly on the back of an envelope.

'But I've done CBT and it didn't really help me.' I'm a bit embarrassed by my plaintive tone.

'That's okay. I still think it's worth trying. It takes some work, but if you're not at your job any more it might be a good way to focus your thoughts and keep building on those positives. You are still doing the yoga, aren't you?'

I nod again. 'I've got some YouTube "yoga for pregnancy" videos. I do twenty minutes twice a day.'

'You see, that's great! You're motivated, you're disciplined. That will really help your recovery. And with the CBT, I think you'll feel better soon. I also think getting that scan will settle things for you a bit. So, what if I see you again at the end of January? You'll have had it by then, won't you?'

'Yes.' My mind is racing, but I can't find words. Is that all? I want to ask. A prescription for a self-help book? I glance at the page of notes he's made, which he's pushed towards me unintentionally. It's full of positives aside from the 'mild depressive symptoms' and 'anxiety' he's documented.

With a big sweep of his hand and a toss of his head, he motions me out of the door. 'All the best then, and have a great Christmas. Joanna will keep in touch with you in the meantime. Goodbye!'

I want to protest. I don't feel heard. I feel a tear escape my left eye.

* * *

'Are you done, love?'

I barely look at Rob as I walk past him towards the car. Strangely, though, I feel some sense of relief. I had expected things to escalate, maybe even the Home Treatment Team to be involved to give me extra support as a pregnant person with schizoaffective disorder. Instead, I'm a slightly over-anxious expectant mum with a prescription for a self-help book.

Rob asks me if I'm okay. I push my hair back from my face and sigh. 'I'm not sure. It wasn't what I expected.'

My appointment with Dr King certainly wasn't what I was used to. Newly arrived from London to take up his first locum consultant position, he had a different approach.

I had come with a shopping list of symptoms: depression, anxiety, worry about being able to look after my baby . . . I had expected him to address them one by one, probably with medication adjustments and possibly an increase in other supports, just as had so often happened previously.

But Dr King wasn't focused on symptoms. That was how a traditional model worked, and he was working within a recovery-focused framework, focusing on my strengths. Rather than looking at the dose of antidepressant or having a conversation about safe tranquillisers to use in pregnancy, he wanted to affirm my ability to manage housework despite low mood, to commend me for using yoga to reduce stress levels, and to empower me through initiating self-help behaviours.

Dr King was building on Dr Ivanov's foundation. Both took a long-term view, with recovery in mind. I'm ashamed to say that I didn't even keep the piece of paper with the name of the CBT book on it. The change in approach to my care was profound, and it took me by surprise – so much so that I needed a few days to digest what had just happened to me. However, the seed Dr King had planted about using self-directed approaches (alongside professional input) soon grew, and I found I was researching helpful books for myself.

Something clicked for me in the weeks that followed. I realised this young doctor's ideas were similar to the ideas I had encountered through the recovery college. It was the first time outside of the college that a health professional had used the word 'recovery' in relation to my journey.

By the time I had my next appointment, I was using the word for myself.

A scan, a book launch and a change in diet

Three significant things happened in January 2020 that helped me to make strides towards this recovery.

The first, early in the month, was my so-called 'twelve-week scan' (which was actually scheduled for my fourteenth week of pregnancy), at the first antenatal appointment. The emotions Rob and I experienced as we met our tiny baby for the first time, heard his heartbeat and watched him kick were indescribable.

Carrying him, I felt as though I already knew our little one, even though I had yet to feel movement. Now I could see him, and the relief at knowing that his heart was beating regularly and at an appropriate rate, and that everything looked healthy, was overwhelming. I smiled and laughed and felt tears well up within me, and I couldn't wait to finally tell my friends we were expecting.

For Rob, it seemed to be even more emotional. Until then, he hadn't really connected with our baby, and he had found it hard to digest the reality of the pregnancy. Not having felt the sickness, the tiredness or the maternal bond, he felt as if he was realising for the first time that this tiny, moving, living being was his child. He couldn't help crying with joy as we clasped each other's hands and watched the ultrasound screen.

I knew that day that I had to do anything – *anything* – that was necessary to recover from my mental illness and be well enough to look after this little person. I had thought I was committed to recovery when I had been discharged from hospital in July, but I had wavered. At this point I decided to focus 100% of my energy on getting, and staying, mentally healthy.

I told Rob this, and promised that – regardless of whether all my health professionals were on board with recovery-focused care or not – I was going to seek whatever support I could get to move forward towards wholeness. Together, we committed to parenting our baby to the best of our ability, and began to pray for him (of course, we didn't know it was a 'him', but it's easier to write that now that we do) in earnest.

It was also at this time that I recognised mental health services would be involved to support me as an individual, but they would not be there to help me parent. It became clear that I would need to prove my own capability as a mother. I redoubled my efforts.

The second thing that happened in January 2020 was that we launched the memoir of my illness and God's goodness to me amid the suffering, *Wrestling with My Thoughts*. This was exciting, and the realisation of a lot of hard work, but it was also another challenge to me in recovery. I had written of my discovery that God is good; that even if he permits me to suffer mental illness, he holds me in his right hand; that even when I feel as though I am floundering, he gives me strength to persevere.

Together with the team at IVP, my publisher, I staged two launch events where I spoke about these truths, and this led to other speaking engagements and appearances on the radio and on various podcasts. My struggles, and the truths I had discovered to help me, were very public, and my healthcare team took note.

I could no longer appear before a nurse utterly helpless; I needed to live up to what I had written. I needed to avoid just saying, 'I'm struggling,' and instead say, 'I may be struggling, but I'm drawing strength from my compassionate God.' Not just, 'This is hard,' but, 'This is hard, and God is good.' My baby and my written testimony were together pushing me towards recovery-focused life choices and recovery-focused word choices.

Then something else happened that helped me towards recovery in an entirely unexpected way. A few weeks later, I was admitted to the surgical ward of a local hospital with an exacerbation of a condition I'd had all my life called colonic dysmotility (a nice way of saying that, because my colon doesn't seem to have a normal nerve supply, it doesn't contract, leaving me with recurrent and severe constipation).

Aside from the fifteen mental health unit admissions since I'd been married, I'd had about a dozen shorter admissions to surgical units, where I'd had to undergo colonic washouts under anaesthetic, and swallow litres of foul-tasting bowel-cleansing drinks while fasting and on IV fluids. It had been at best disruptive, and at worst painful, nauseating and dangerous, as the electrolytes in my blood swung out of balance, putting my heart at risk.

There is a lot of research and discussion about the 'gut-brain axis' these days, and the impact that gastrointestinal problems can have on mental health. I have no doubt that, painfully bloated, toxins in my system and bacterial overgrowth in my bowel did affect my mental health directly, but for me, the obvious effects on wellbeing came from repeated admissions to hospital. This often meant that I could not access support from mental health services, and on a few occasions I had to be moved from an inpatient mental health unit to a surgical ward in a state of acute psychiatric distress.

This admission, early in 2020, was my first while pregnant, and I was sure that it would not be my last. I was wrong. The fact that I was pregnant complicated matters because the usual course of action when I presented with a swollen tummy was to X-ray the abdomen to check that the bowel was not completely obstructed. An X-ray could have harmed my baby, so the surgical team had to rely on other clues.

Thankfully, there was no obstruction, so I could be treated conservatively. I was introduced to a very young dietitian with a specialism in gastrointestinal disorders. She suggested that, rather than eating the high-fibre diet that had been my norm for so many years, I ought to try a low-residue diet (which should only be undertaken with the advice of a specialist health professional). I would reduce the load of difficult-to-digest fruits and vegetables, replace brown bread and pasta with white, and eat cornflakes or Rice Krispies for breakfast.

Within a couple of days of making the changes, I saw results. Instead of trying to force an inert bowel to contract against fibrous residue, the new diet allowed easy transit and meant that I had a whole lot less digesting to do in general. I still had to take medication to keep water in my gut and to stimulate it, but the transformation was incredible.

While 2019 broke the cycle of psychiatric admissions, 2020 broke the cycle of surgical admissions. Life suddenly became easier and more predictable, and I felt much healthier. It also removed another worry from my pregnancy – about what would happen if I needed bowel surgery, which had always been a risk for me.

By the time my next review with Dr King came around, I felt as though I was in a good place mentally, physically and spiritually.

A psychological shift

I had continued to work hard with Debbie throughout this time, and one thing we had talked a lot about was identity. I realised that, for the past fifteen years, I had identified strongly as a sick person; specifically as a mentally ill person. I really felt that I wanted to leave the sick role behind and focus on my roles as a wife and mother, and – having just launched my book – as a writer.

It felt like a big shift, and it was scary. So much of my security had come from the supports that were in place for me precisely because I was sick. But I had a lightbulb moment when I realised the most important aspect of my identity was a constant: that I was a child of God whether I was sick or well, whether I was living on my own or as part of a family. I had to trust that God would provide all the support I needed, even if this might not be directly through the mental health team.

This was vitally important because, from that first antenatal appointment, I faced questions as to whether I was well enough to parent a child. In particular, there were concerns about the severity of my depression and the risks of my becoming psychotic. I knew that I was going to have to prove my fitness to be a mum to this baby, and it added to my resolve to recover.

By this stage, my prayer life was changing. Rather than shooting up 'arrow prayers' to ask for help with my current mood or for strength to get through until I next saw my nurse, I was thinking more of the longer-term when I prayed, asking for help and strength for recovery.

When I saw Dr King this time, I was no longer aghast that he didn't seem to be taking my concerns seriously enough. Instead, I was enormously grateful that he had classified my depression – now lifted – as mild, and that he had normalised my anxiety as typical of any first-time mother. He was able to confirm that I'd had no episodes of psychosis and that, in his view, I was an averagely well pregnant mum.

The next milestone for Rob and me was the 'big scan', as it was known: the twenty-week anomaly scan when we would find out if there were any identifiable issues with our baby's health, and when we would learn whether we were to have a boy or a girl. It was particularly significant for us because we had decided that I needed to keep taking my medications throughout pregnancy, and it was not yet known whether two of these posed any risk to an unborn child.

As it turned out, the sonographer had a fantastic view. Baby was lying at just the right angle to show his facial profile, and we soon had a printout of his tiny features, including a cute little turned-up nose! It was hard to miss that we were having a boy, too, and I remember suddenly feeling that this was exactly what I wanted – even though I had felt up to this point that I didn't care whether it was to be a boy or a girl, as long as they were healthy.

Watching our wakeful son kicking and punching, our joy was complete when the scan was finished and we were told that everything looked absolutely normal. He was growing exactly as expected for his gestation. We had chosen names for a girl and a boy, and from this point forward we were able to talk about our little one by name. I remember we laughed together and held each other close as we listened to the strong beat of his heart. We just couldn't wait to meet him!

New anxieties

But it was at this appointment that I also had to meet with a midwife who would educate me about health issues in pregnancy, for both me and our baby. It was here that I first heard about foetal movements, and how critical it was for me to learn my baby's patterns: the times of day when he was most active, and whether he was generally a bit lazy or a bit hyperactive. I learned that changes to his patterns, and particularly reduced levels of movement, could mean that he was not doing well, and that, if this happened, I needed to contact the emergency obstetric unit (EOU) so he could be assessed.

This proved to be the start of another journey for me, with new anxieties that would be present until the day our baby finally arrived. I had only just begun to feel the first flutters of movement at twenty weeks. By the time another week had passed, I began to worry if I hadn't felt movement for a few hours. I made my first call to the EOU at just twenty-one weeks because baby seemed to have been still all day.

On this occasion, a cardiotocography scan (CTG), used to measure foetal heartrate (as well as uterine contractions), soon gave us a clean bill of health. The midwife at the EOU showed me the little peaks in the tracing when baby's heartrate had accelerated. This should happen at least twice every twenty minutes, indicating that baby was moving around even when I couldn't feel him.

My anxieties eased, and I got on with life for a week or two, until again I had a prolonged period when I felt nothing. I attended the EOU again. Again, the CTG was fine; again, I settled, relieved that baby was doing okay.

However, by twenty-eight weeks I still couldn't recognise a pattern to baby's movements, and was going hours without feeling anything. The midwives reassured me that I could never call too often about reduced foetal movements (I soon recognised another three-letter abbreviation on my charts: RFM, which stood for reduced foetal movements, but actually related more to the mother's perception of reduced movement than the medical reality), and that they would much rather have ongoing false alarms than miss a possible problem.

I started to worry that my anxiety would impact on other areas of my mental health, and I know this was a concern for the health professionals involved. Thankfully, my mood stayed buoyant, and I never descended into panic and paranoia. It just meant that Rob and I regularly spent a night at EOU: me inside with a CTG monitor attached to my growing bump; Rob having to sit outside in his car because of new Covid-19 regulations.

And sometimes the midwives were a bit concerned. On several of the occasions when I was there, there were no accelerations on the CTG for almost an hour. However, by the time the consultant was called, baby was always bopping about, with accelerations occurring almost every minute! I was told I just had a sleepy, relaxed baby. Still, I felt the need to count the kicks for an hour almost every day, just to be sure, and drank endless glasses of iced fruit juice to stimulate baby when I could feel nothing.

The staff in EOU were also the first to recognise that my blood pressure was becoming elevated to alarming levels, and this led to an admission to the maternity ward, when I was put on an anti-hypertensive. That evening, I remember feeling extremely upset because I overheard a midwife on the phone to the on-call obstetrician. She said: 'The schizophrenic woman's blood pressure is 170 over 107.' I no longer wanted to be identified as a mentally ill person; I was first and foremost an expectant mum, and to add insult to injury she hadn't even got my psychiatric diagnosis right!

But my obstetrician was dismissive when I told him about it, saying it was normal for health professionals to use shorthand when communicating about patients, and that I shouldn't be worried. For me, though, it was stigmatising, and until you have felt stigmatised yourself it is hard to understand how dehumanising it is.

Motivations to recover

All the while this was going on, I still managed to enjoy my pregnancy. I remember our excitement the first time Rob was able to put his hand on my tummy and feel baby moving. I remember the fun we had planning our baby shower, which had to happen via Zoom because we were in lockdown.

Dr King moved on, and a friendly Nigerian psychiatrist, Dr Musa, took over. By this stage in the pandemic, consultations were happening via Zoom, and I was nervous about our first meeting, but he put me entirely at ease. I liked him straight away, and he was very positive about my progress in recovery – carefully documenting that I was mentally well, and taking the view that my anxieties about foetal movement were not unusual in a pregnant mum.

At this point, he was also asked to document the probable risk of my developing perinatal psychosis, given that I had been psychotic in the past. He was very positive, saying – given that I was still taking antipsychotics and had been well so far in pregnancy – that I would probably not become psychotic. However, he still felt the risk to be around 20%. This was obviously a concern, but I just wanted to focus even more on doing all I could to continue with my recovery. After all, it meant there was an 80% chance I would remain well.

I was reading about recovery and talking to my mental health team about it when I came across the concept of recovery as a balance of acceptance (of ongoing symptoms) and change (making adjustments to life to promote recovery wherever possible). I recognised that I was becoming good at implementing changes, such as making sure that I got plenty of sunlight every day and committing to never missing one of my twice-daily, twenty-minute pregnancy yoga sessions.

I was less capable of accepting ongoing symptoms: the anxieties I felt, the tiredness associated with antipsychotics, my increasingly heavy frame and my difficulty in finding a comfortable sleeping position. This acceptance would come later in my journey.

My aunt, Olivia, said to me one day: 'I've been frustrated with you before, because as soon as things have got hard with whatever you're doing, you've ducked out. Well, there's no ducking with this one.'

I was going to have a baby and I needed to be well and to persevere, regardless of how I felt about it.

Later, she would say: 'It's been tough, but you haven't ducked. I'm proud of you.'

That meant more to me than she could ever understand.

Perinatal mental illness

Perinatal mental illness refers to any maternal mental health problem that occurs from conception to one year after birth.[2] Perinatal mental health issues are the most common complication of childbearing. The incidence of postnatal depression is around 12% and postnatal anxiety around 10%.[3] Perinatal psychosis (loss of touch with reality) is much rarer, with only around 1 in 500 women experiencing it.[4]

Studies show that perinatal psychosis is much more common than this in women with a pre-existing severe mental illness. I have schizoaffective disorder (bipolar type), and women with bipolar disorder have been shown to have a 20% risk.[5] For women who have had one episode of perinatal psychosis, the risk of recurrence with another baby is as high as 50%.[6]

Postnatal depression is usually treatable, often with extra social support, talking therapies (such as cognitive behavioural therapy) and antidepressant drugs.[7] Postpartum psychosis is a medical emergency requiring hospitalisation, preferably in a special psychiatric mother and baby unit, and treatment with antipsychotic drugs (and/or mood stabilisers and antidepressants). With the right treatment and support, most mothers make a full recovery, though this can take time.[8]

Of course, all new mums experience hormonal changes, sleep deprivation, and often a few days of 'baby blues', so feeling a range of emotions is totally normal.[9] Support from friends and family – and a church – is always needed around this time. If a mum or someone close to her suspects she may have a more significant mental health problem, these supporters can assist her in accessing professional help.

If someone has a pre-existing mental illness, as I did, planning for pregnancy can make a real difference, as it is possible to reduce the risk of perinatal mental health problems. For example, women who choose to keep taking their antipsychotic medication, thought to be safe in pregnancy, are much less likely to become unwell than those who come off their drugs.[10]

Many women are anxious about reporting symptoms of mental illness because they fear that people will think they are unable to look after their babies, yet it's vitally important that they get the support they need.[11] Perinatal mental illness poses risks to the mother (suicide accounts for up to 20% of maternal deaths), and to the baby, whose physical and mental health may be affected (and for whom, in cases of psychosis, there is a risk of direct harm).[12]

For these reasons, I believe we need to talk more about these conditions, raise awareness and thereby help to reduce stigma.

Scripture and reflection

Strengths, weaknesses and putting one foot in front of the other

Working on recovery-focused principles, Dr King concentrated on my strengths. I was disciplined and motivated, and was keeping up the basics in life – housework and meal preparation – despite my mood being lower than I would have liked.

The recovery model would also recognise the fact that I have a faith as a strength (although I don't recall sharing this with Dr King at the time). Any kind of spirituality that might be helpful to someone in their recovery is valued by recovery practitioners, including a Christian faith, whether they share it or not. This presents an opportunity for churches to be involved in supporting those on a recovery journey.

As a Christian, I can see these strengths as God-given, but they are only a starting point. I want to reiterate that recovery is not about 'pulling oneself up by one's bootstraps'. It is important to build on strengths and channel them for recovery, but I must be aware of my weaknesses and allow God to work in my life at my weakest points.

I went to Dr King with the wrong attitude, completely focused on my low mood and anxieties, and expecting him to 'fix' them for me, one by one. In time, and with prayer, I was able to shift my perspective.

I spent time reading Paul's letter to the Corinthians, where he described asking the Lord three times to take away a condition from which he suffered – a 'thorn in my flesh' (2 Corinthians 12:7), as he called it. Jesus' reply was: 'My grace is sufficient for you, for my power is made perfect in weakness' (12:9). Paul's response was to boast of his weaknesses. He concluded: 'That is why, for Christ's sake, I delight in weaknesses . . . For when I am weak, then I am strong' (12:10).

In the recovery model, the expectation is not that the mental illness will be 'cured'. The 'thorn in the flesh' may never be removed. I will most likely have episodes of mental ill health for the rest of my life. However, there is an expectation that *quality of life* will improve if a patient invests in positive experiences.

As a Christian, I can invest in the positive things in my life. I can also lean in to the difficult things, because it is here, in my weakness, that God's power is made perfect. When I wrote *Wrestling with My Thoughts,* I was very aware of this. I was not yet in recovery, and I was very weak indeed, but I knew that Christ's grace was sufficient. Now, even more so, I can say that 'when I am weak, then I am strong'. I am proving God's power through my recovery. Of course, Paul did not feel glorious in every waking moment. He endured great hardships during his ministry: beatings, imprisonment and riots; hard work, sleepless nights and hunger (2 Corinthians 6:5). He must often have been exhausted, ill and in pain. But crucially, he kept on going, step by step . . . by step . . . by step.

In 1 Timothy 6:12, he gives a final charge to his protégé, Timothy, telling him to: 'Fight the good fight of the faith.' He likens the faith journey to a battle. Timothy must keep on going, fighting day by day, even when he feels he is spent. Paul writes again to Timothy as the end of his life draws near: 'I have fought the good fight, I have finished the race, I have kept the faith' (2 Timothy 4:7).

The writer to the Hebrews also uses the analogy of the faith journey as a long-distance race. He urges us to 'run with perseverance the race marked out for us' (12:1).

I used to compete in the 3,000-metre race when I was at school. Finishing well required certain tactics and good physical fitness, but I found that the single factor that made the most impact on my performance was psychological stamina. When the going got tough, I had to keep putting one foot in front of the other.

I am on a faith journey. It is a battle. It is a long-distance race. My faith journey and my recovery journey are, in many ways, one and the same thing. Like Paul, I move forward with a 'thorn in my flesh'. Various theologians have speculated about what Paul's thorn was, but we cannot be sure. For me, the thorn in my flesh is schizo-affective disorder.

Every day, I must utilise my God-given strengths and find Christ's power in my weakness to keep moving forward in faith and recovery. Most of the time it is the simple act of putting one foot in front of the other that stops me from capitulating in battle or dropping out of the race. And there is always sufficient grace for that single next step. Always. Step . . . by step . . . by step . . . I will finish the race.

Questions for personal reflection or discussion

1. Have you ever felt taken aback by a change in approach to your mental healthcare or that of someone you care about? What was the outcome?
2. What is it that keeps you running the race of faith and/or recovery? Is there anything that causes you to step off the track?

4

Deep growth

Encountering God, examining myself

'Whatever you do, do it as unto the Lord.'
(Colossians 3:23)

Recovery principle 6
'Recovery encompasses an individual's whole life, including mind, body, spirit, and community.'

'Wholeness in Old Testament perspective is not perfection, nor does it consist in some ideal state of well-being. Rather, in biblical modelling, it inhabits the space between reality and the hoped-for perfection of all things. Wholeness is a practice in which human fragility is fully self-aware, but finds a context in belonging and love, in the "social body", in shared memory, and in the community's affirmations of the faith.'[1]
(Professor Gordon McConville)

So many false starts

Pregnancy presented me with an opportunity. By the start of the second trimester I had given up my job as a paralegal, but I still had six months left before life was set to change for ever: from July I would be a mum, and I intended to focus wholly on our baby for at least his first year. I started to think – and pray – about how I might use this time well. Little did I know that I was about to have a lot more time on my hands, as the UK went into lockdown six weeks later.

I thought back over the past few years, and further, to the various endeavours I had pursued. I've written of my failed efforts to complete courses in beauty therapy and proofreading. There were also many other false starts, including jobs in a coffee shop and a hairdressing salon (both of which I left after one day); a banking job I quit before I had completed the initial training; short stints on gardening and customer service courses run by a local mental health charity; and an apprenticeship at the BBC, where I only lasted two weeks.

Repeated failures across such a vast spectrum had left me feeling hopeless and embarrassed, and my CV made me appear chaotic, unfocused and completely unreliable (as perhaps I was).

I felt that there were three reasons why I had not been able to go the distance on any of these occasions. First, my medications were far from optimal and were being continually changed, so I just didn't have a stable chemical 'brain environment'. I was also dipping in and out of various talking therapies, none of which seemed particularly effective, and some of which destabilised me.

Second, psychologically speaking, I was still mired in the 'sick role'. This meant that as soon as I felt unwell at college or at work, I felt licensed to give up and go home. I had a severe mental illness, after all, so I couldn't really be expected to keep studying or hold down a job.

Third, I had tried each of these pursuits with flawed motivation. I was trying to 'work myself well'; to find the course or job that would provide a route out of illness, telling myself that if I could just find my niche, I would feel at peace. It wasn't true, of course. I needed to recover before I could find my niche; I needed to establish my values and then pursue a life that lined up with them, not find a way of life that seemed 'valid' and line my values up to suit it.

Throughout this time I was very driven by the need to prove myself to other people, to do something I thought they would see as valid and worthwhile – rather than simply seeing me as mentally ill and incapable. So there had to be a pay packet at the end of whatever I pursued, or at least the certification that might ultimately lead to gainful employment.

Once when I had just left one of these courses, I remember Olivia saying to me, 'I wish you would stop running away.' Formidable but wonderfully warmhearted, she was often frustrated by my tendency to give up when things got hard. I really wanted to show her I could stick with something, but pre-recovery it seemed impossible.

A drooping flower

I have already made reference to the 'recovery flower' developed by psychologist and recovery campaigner Dr Deegan. She described a simple flower with a centre and petals to represent a person with a mental illness. Pre-recovery, the centre of the flower represents the illness or the diagnosis, with the petals representing other aspects of the person and their lives: hobbies, interests, relationships and so forth. Once recovery begins the illness is displaced, becoming just one petal among many. The centre represents the person herself: her personality and key characteristics.

I realise now, as I look back on all these desperate, frantic efforts to find the right job or course to suit me, that what I was really trying to do was displace my schizoaffective disorder diagnosis from the centre of my flower – to find a new identity, be that as a beauty therapist or a barista. The problem was that, time and time again, these new identities merely became petals attached to the central illness . . . and sooner or later they died and fell off altogether.

My efforts were characterised by a sense of urgency. Once I had come across a job or course I thought might be a good fit, I had to apply for it that very day, as I was always scared I would get ill again or lose motivation and miss out on an opportunity to escape my illness. Once things got hard on that course or in that job, it became just as urgent for me to leave it. I couldn't tough it out for a few weeks to see if I might overcome my difficulties – I had to quit there and then.

During that first 2020 lockdown, as I looked once more at choosing what to do during the second half of my pregnancy, life felt very much less urgent. There were several reasons for this. I had achieved something concrete in the form of my book, which I knew others saw as a worthwhile, valid endeavour. I could say that I was an author. I was also soon to become a mum, surely another valid role.

But there was something much more profound going on. I had embraced recovery, and at last my schizoaffective disorder had shifted from the centre of my flower to become a petal. What's more, I had not replaced it with 'author' or 'mother', although those had become other, very important, petals.

When Dr Deegan drew her flower, at the centre was simply 'Pat', representing all her personality traits and idiosyncrasies with her schizophrenia as a petal, her job as a psychologist as another, and so on. I had 'Sharon' at the centre, but I could take the illustration a step further. The stem was my identity as a child of God, and my flower was 'rooted and established in [Christ's] love' (Ephesians 3:17).

This recognition that the most important aspect of my person-hood was not what I did but to whom I belonged (something my counsellor and I worked very hard on) was an incredible landmark on my journey to recovery. It put an end to my exhausting strivings and changed me from a human *doing* to a human *being*.

With this other tiny human being growing inside me, I saw God's father heart from a new vantage point: that of a parent. I could imagine him quietening me, encouraging me and loving me exactly as I was – in the same gentle way that I related to my little son.

I'd had a living relationship with God for years, and it had always been a significant and important part of my life, but it had only ever been a single – albeit bright – petal on my flower. As I thought about recovery and embraced it fully, I realised that the head of my flower had been drooping for much of my adult life. I knew that the only way for it to bloom healthily was to draw strength from my roots in his love through the stem of my identity in him.

Pursuing a deeper theology

I had been reading devotionals and books on Christian living consistently and earnestly alongside my Bible since childhood, though there had been many rough spells during my illness when I could barely manage more than a verse at a time. I had a reasonable knowledge of many passages of Scripture, and my repertoire of childhood memory verses had served me well when it came to writing *Wrestling with My Thoughts* and needing to highlight certain biblical truths.

However, I had long realised that my knowledge of the Bible as a whole entity was patchy. I remember a family member quoting Jeremiah 29:11 to me once ("'For I know the plans I have for you," declares the Lord, "plans to prosper you and not to harm you, plans to give you hope and a future'"), relating it to the desired improvement in my mental health. When I told a friend about this, she pointed out that God promised seventy years of exile before this came to fruition!

I think that was a key moment for me. I knew many verses from the Bible, but was lacking in understanding of their contexts. I wanted this to change. That's why, in 2018, I had started my graduate diploma in Theology. As I wrote in a previous chapter, this was the first course I took where I really felt as though I had landed on something important.

Of course, 2018 was pre-recovery, and I had to withdraw. But at this point, in 2020, I knew I wanted to revisit that field of study. I was talking about this one day with Olivia when she told me about a website she had stumbled upon called 'Biblical Training' (www.biblicaltraining.org), which offered free access to seminary courses.

I looked it up and was struck by an endorsement from Christian author, speaker and radio host Joni Eareckson Tada, who had become a quadriplegic following a diving accident, aged seventeen. She said that Biblical Training opened the doors of seminaries to those with disabilities. Joni, who founded Joni and Friends, an international Christian ministry to the disabled, had been a heroine of mine since reading her mini-biography as a six-year-old! On seeing her endorsement, I thought, *Well, I'm someone with a disability. Maybe this is worth checking out.*

I approached this opportunity with a totally different mindset: a recovery-focused mindset. I was not going to take a Biblical

Training course to get accreditation or to earn a diploma. These were free lecture series from courses offered across the US, but there was no option to submit work or receive feedback. I no longer needed to do something that other people would consider valid; it was enough that I felt sure God would think it a valid use of my time, and I truly believed that learning theology would advance my recovery. By then, this was a huge motivator.

So it was that I enrolled for an Old Testament Survey course recommended as a foundational module. I told Rob what I was doing, although I imagine his expectations were low. I had a bad track record. I explained that this was different. I was doing it because I wanted to understand God better.

An eye-opening experience

My intention was to read the entire Old Testament alongside this course, and, if there was still time before baby arrived, to follow this with a New Testament Survey, meaning I would read the Bible in its entirety during my pregnancy. And this is what I did. It helped that I had more time than I had expected, as once we were in lockdown I no longer travelled to Belfast for weekly counselling appointments (we used Zoom instead); coffee dates were impossible; and all my book-related speaking engagements were cancelled.

I started listening to the audio Bible through earphones when walking the dogs, and during long, sunny lockdown afternoons when Rob and I were working on various projects in the garden (he, doing hard physical labour; me, slowly painting sheds, fences, decking and plant pots). And each time I completed a book, I spent a few mornings indoors listening to the corresponding lectures via the Biblical Training website.

I found the experience truly eye-opening. I realised I hadn't understood very much of the Bible at all. I had known that there were different genres of biblical literature: history, poetry, wisdom, prophecy, and so on, but I hadn't known how they fitted together. I knew in a woolly sort of way that the prophetic books followed on from history in the Old Testament. I don't think I had ever fully realised that the prophets spoke to God's people during the periods of history recorded. I thought they came afterwards.

So, what did I learn? Bear with me if I get a little technical for a paragraph or two. I realise that some readers may know little of the Bible, but I would like to spell out what I learned in the language of theology.

First, that Moses' five books of the law, the Pentateuch at the start of the Old Testament, record patriarchal history from creation and the first stories of man (generally thought to be around 6,000 years ago), through the story of Abraham and his descendants to the time of Joshua and the Israelites' entry to the Promised Land.

Second, that this was followed by two phases of human leadership, under God: first through the judges (from c. 1400–1000 BC), and then the kings (c. 1000–586 BC) . . . and that 1 and 2 Kings and 1 and 2 Chronicles tell the same history, but for different audiences.

Third, that Jerusalem fell in 586 and there followed a seventy-year period of exile (when most of God's people were captured and taken to Babylon), before they were allowed to return and the Temple was restored. Beyond this restoration, what we know of the history of the Jewish people up to the time of Jesus' birth comes from the post-exilic prophets and other sources. There is a gap in the history told in the Bible between c. 400 BC and the birth of Christ.

If this all seems very dry and complicated, I have to say that, for me, it was anything but; it was as if all the bits and pieces of books and verses I was so familiar with were suddenly falling into place. It probably seems very strange that someone who had spent a lifetime in church, Bible classes and small group studies (preceded, during childhood, by Sunday school and other youth organisations) would not have this kind of knowledge and understanding, but the Bible had simply never been presented to me in this way. I had only studied individual books and themes.

I knew about King David, and that he had been a man after God's own heart (1 Samuel 13:14; Acts 13:22), despite some terrible wrongdoings. I didn't know that he reigned from c. 1010–970 BC, having some vague idea that he had lived much longer ago. I had no timeline in my head along which to place him. I knew there had been at least one period during which the Jewish people lived in exile, but I didn't know when and had again thought it was deep in the mists of time.

Once I had a handle on the sequence of events, the Bible seemed a lot simpler to understand. I thought I had missed out on lots of important events because I hadn't read the Bible as a whole during adulthood. In reality, I was familiar with almost all of the stories I encountered on this reading, but had no framework from which to hang them.

I began to learn how to read the different types of literature by understanding the writers and their audiences; to read passages from similar time periods side by side; and to begin to understand the arc of history, with God's old and new covenant agreements – through the law, and then through Jesus the Saviour – for the first time.

The character of God

To be honest, I had been a little nervous about delving into the Old Testament. I could hear the voice of one of my former psychologists in my head: 'How can you believe that the God of the Old Testament is the same God you read about in the New Testament? I've read both, and Jesus is attractive, but don't you think God was capricious and vengeful – inciting so-called "holy wars" where not even the women and children were spared, and demanding all these burned animals to keep himself satisfied?'

I remember feeling unsettled. I didn't understand – or like – the idea of wars in which no one was spared, and I'm a pescatarian, so have felt uneasy about animal sacrifice since my teens. I tried to respond to him, 'B-b-but he was the same. It was a different context . . . ' And I think I tried to paraphrase words found in several places in the Old Testament, such as: 'The LORD is gracious and compassionate, slow to anger and rich in love' (Psalm 145:8).

That was how I wanted to find the God of the Old Testament. Was it possible that I would encounter a capricious, vengeful God?

I didn't, of course. It took me a while to get my head around the concept of holy war (on which I found several lectures within my course material), and I did find a God who showed righteous anger. But I found consistency within his character rather than caprice, justness rather than vengeance.

The God I met in the Old Testament was a creative, relational, loving being. A God with many emotions – though, unlike me, in full command of all of them. He was a covenant God, a God who made, and kept, promises to his people. A God who acted on the agreements he made with them, to bless them, and who disciplined them when they broke them. As I read on, I realised that God did, at times, look away from his people, but never for too long. He promised a Messiah – a Saviour – through the genetic line of King David, and this was never in doubt.

I found a God who was holy, which the Merriam-Webster dictionary defines as 'exalted or worthy of complete devotion as one perfect in goodness and righteousness'.[2] The Hebrew word is *qodesh*, which means 'set apart', 'sacred'.[3] I do still sometimes struggle with why animal sacrifices – and eventually Jesus' ultimate sacrifice – were necessary, but I now understand that blood and its shedding were highly significant within Jewish culture, and that the ceremonies around the Temple and sacrificial rites reflected and reinforced the holiness of God. He could not look on sin and tolerate it, and there had to be atonement for the wrongs of mankind.

Rather than a vengeful God, I found a jealous God. Jealousy has negative connotations for us, of course, but we humans have no right to be jealous. God, on the other hand, rightly wanted all his people's worship and was rightly jealous when they turned to idols. I came to understand that idol worship (for example of the Baals, for whom his people so often forsook him) saddened God terribly. He could not tolerate it, and sometimes wars were needed to eradicate it. I thought about how often we make modern-day idols and how jealous and sad this must make God today.

I met an eternal God; an omniscient (all-seeing) and omnipresent (everywhere-at-the-same-time) God; a God whose wrath was always justified; a God who listens to his people and speaks to them; a God who is pure; a God who is understanding. In short, I met the 'gracious and compassionate, slow to anger and rich in love' God I had vaguely tried to defend to my former psychologist. How much better equipped I would be to counter him if I saw him again today!

Of course, aside from meeting God, I found a lot of striking things in the Old Testament: the voices of lament, which gave me new avenues to express my pain in times of depression and difficulty; the messianic prophecies (and prophecies reaching beyond even the present day) in the context of the Hebrew Scriptures (reading *The Bible Jesus Read* by Philip Yancey (Zondervan, 2001) alongside the Old Testament helped me here); and the incredible poetry to be found in many ancient Scriptures, from Job to Isaiah. My encounter with God was life-changing and had a huge impact on my recovery journey.

Moving forward in faith and recovery

In *Wrestling with My Thoughts*, I wrote of my threefold recognition that God is good (Psalm 13:6), that he holds me (Psalm 139:10) and that he gives me strength (Psalm 46:1). Since childhood, I had prayed to this God as my '*Abba*, Father' (Mark 14:36), following the pattern presented by Jesus himself in the Gospels. I knew it was a term of intimacy; I had even heard it translated as 'Daddy'. There was a new layer of meaning to 'Abba' for me now that I was to become a parent myself. Even this tiny child growing inside me had generated a fierce, passionate, protective love I had never felt before. And God felt that for me? It was incredible.

My reading of the Old Testament didn't negate any of this. Instead, it confirmed everything I had learned previously but put it into a wider context. The God who was good was also majestic; the God who held me was also perfect in holiness; the God who gave me strength also ruled the universe with power and might. My Father God was a covenant God; a God who demands obedience as well as inspiring trust.

I knew that I needed to change my posture before God in light of what I was discovering. Of course, I still believe it is possible to pray to God in any situation and that he wants me to come as I am, bringing my cares and my woes, presenting my requests before him (Philippians 4:6). I believe he is accessible (Ephesians 2:18); I believe the Spirit intercedes when all I can do is groan (Romans 8:26); I believe I can show him my emotions (as demonstrated in the psalms). I do not believe I *have* to prostrate myself before God in order for him to hear me, but reading the Old Testament made me *want* to come with a greater sense of awe. I wanted to prepare myself to meet with him; I wanted to have the right attitude before him; I wanted to use words that conveyed my respect for his majesty.

I remember one evening I was listening to some contemporary Christian music and one song helped these things fall into place for me. It was the late Rich Mullins' recording of 'Awesome God', released when I was just six years old and something of an inter-mittent soundtrack for my life ever since. It speaks of a God who is awesome and who reigns from heaven with wisdom, power and love. As the music played, I took the words as my own.

This and another song, 'Agnus Dei' by Michael W. Smith – with lyrics based on verses from the New Testament book of Revelation (4:8; 5:12) – played in my head on repeat as I formulated my own prayer: 'Lord God Almighty, you are holy, holy, holy. You are worthy to receive power and wealth and wisdom and strength and honour and glory and praise!'

Just before lockdown, Rob and I had been to a rehearsed reading of the complete book of Revelation, performed by Revd Professor Gordon Campbell at Union Theological College, where I had pre-viously begun my graduate diploma. It had brought the holiness of heaven to life for me, and now the experience made more sense, in that I knew the holy God of the Old Testament, who remained the holy God of the New Testament, and of the still-to-come events prophesied by John in Revelation.

The change in how I prayed did not come overnight, and is still something of a process. Music still helps. Just this year, I made a publicly shared resolution to pray with more awe, and I recently wrote a blog post in which I admitted that I don't always succeed.

However, I am much less likely to bargain with God or plead with him over things when I know it's really my job to take responsibility to make changes. I have tried to stop presenting him with lists of things to 'fix' for me. I had also been in a habit of repeating little phrases over and over to him in an almost superstitious way, thinking that if I didn't say such and such, something bad would happen. I have been working towards eliminating that practice.

Why do I say that this has made such an impact on my recovery? I think the progress has come from feeling that I am in a better place before God; that I know him better, can relate to him better; that I am humbler before him and more careful in what I say to him. I do find myself taking more responsibility for my wellbeing rather than just handing things over to God, then expecting him to pick up the pieces when I make a mess of things. I think I also trust him more because I have seen his consistency and how he keeps promises; how he is always good, always holding me in his hand, always giving me strength. I know for sure that he is not capricious or vengeful. I am also more confident when I talk about God, because I know the whole Old Testament now and I realise there are no skeletons in God's closet. As the Bible says, 'I AM WHO I AM' (Exodus 3:14).

That all of this impacted on my recovery journey makes sense, considering the CHIME factors I reflected on in chapter 1. I felt more **Connected** with God; I had greater **Hope** in him; I had confirmed my **Identity** in him; relationship with him was giving my life more **Meaning**; and knowing he is so awesome yet offers me strength as his child was **Empowering**.

The further, powerful impact on my recovery came from the simple act of *finishing* the Old Testament Survey course. The only tangible reward may have been the little badge on the Biblical Training website, but for me the intangible rewards were huge. I had such a sense of accomplishment. It felt as though all those false starts with the other courses mattered so much less. I had made it to the end of something, persevering through the tough spots and tired days, and I felt it was evidence of a stickability I hadn't thought myself capable of. I could show Olivia my badge, which could have read: 'Well done – you didn't run away!'

In the recovery model, the process of fulfilling small goals, then using them as a foundation from which to achieve bigger goals is known as 'building mastery'. I really did feel a sense of mastery after reading all thirty-nine books of the Old Testament and listening carefully to all the (sometimes complex) lectures that went alongside it. I didn't need a certificate, diploma or transferable credit to know that I had done something worthwhile. I didn't need greater job prospects. I felt more knowledgeable, certainly, but the most important outcome by far was that I understood the God I had worshipped since childhood so much better.

I did build on this foundation by going on to read the New Testament in its entirety, and I also completed a survey of the four Gospels, which I found fascinating. Again, I realised how little I had known of the context and culture in which Jesus lived, and of the way in which the gospel accounts came together.

I had hoped to begin a survey of the remainder of the New Testament before our baby arrived, but this proved impossible, as the last few weeks of the third trimester were busy, I was tired and heavy (and still having episodes of reduced foetal movement), and in the end my labour was induced after thirty-seven weeks. I hope I will take that course one day, but I felt as though I was bursting with new biblical knowledge, and I was already quite familiar with the epistles of the New Testament, since they had been the subject of many sermon series I had heard and Bible studies I had taken part in.

A long, hard look at myself

All this study allowed me to re-evaluate my perceptions of God. It also prompted me to re-examine myself. I realised that this awesome, holy, pure and righteous God could not look on sin. I knew that Jesus had died and risen again to take away my guilt and shame, but I also knew this was not a reason to keep on sinning. As the writer of Hebrews says emphatically: 'If we deliberately keep on sinning after we have received the knowledge of the truth, no sacrifice for sins is left, but only a fearful expectation of judgment and of raging fire that will consume the enemies of God' (10:26–27).

For some time, I deliberately tried to be more aware of my thoughts and actions throughout the day, identifying moments of sinfulness or wilful disobedience to God. It was not long before something clicked with me that was critical for my recovery: I needed to stop using my illness as an excuse for un-Christlike behaviour.

The one person who has experienced at first hand all the ups and downs of my schizoaffective disorder over the past decade is of course my husband, Rob. He has seen me depressed and sprawled across our bed, crying. He has seen me manic and talking quickfire nonsense. He has seen me cowering in a corner, psychotic and terrified. As I began to really examine myself, I realised he has also borne the brunt of my sinfulness.

Let me be very clear: it is in no way sinful to be mentally ill, manic, psychotic and so on. It is because of the fall that we have mental illness (along with physical illness and every other form of human suffering), but the individual who becomes mentally ill is neither sinful nor being punished for sinfulness. What was wrong in my case was that there were times when I was not displaying the fruits of the Spirit in my life – when I was unkind, impatient, lacking in gentleness – and I was using my mental illness as a justification. I needed to take responsibility, acknowledging that mental illness made it harder for me to be always in control, but aiming towards greater Christlikeness.

I know that Rob would not expect to be portrayed as a saint. He is human, but he has shown tremendous patience with me throughout my changing moods over the years, as well as a fierce loyalty. We have had our differences at times, just like any couple, and it was my reactions to these differences that first came to mind when I started the process of serious self-examination.

I realised that – particularly, but not exclusively, during periods of mental distress – I did not always relate well to Rob. I often expected him to read my mind, and would act out my frustration when he failed to notice I was really struggling or didn't do something I wanted him to do (even though I hadn't told him). I was also quick to overreact to minor misdemeanours that seemed (to me) to threaten my fragile mental state, such as making me ten minutes late for an appointment.

But the single biggest problem I recognised in myself regarding my relationship with Rob was my failure to stay in command of my emotions during our occasional arguments. When I was feeling mentally vulnerable, I tended to think that Rob shouldn't disagree with me because of my vulnerability. I felt he should try to de-escalate tension in difficult discussions rather than insisting he was right and further ramping up the emotion in the moment.

I realised I found it very hard to let go of my own need to be right and could get angry or even scream in exasperation if I felt Rob was wrong and not listening to me. I would then end up apologising, but always with an excuse: 'I couldn't help it – I'm dealing with really agitated depression right now. Didn't you know?' Whether I was being plaintive and helpless, or was experiencing really heightened emotions I didn't have a handle on, I was quick to blame my illness.

Now, I'm not saying this happened all the time. For the most part, Rob and I get on very well and our relationship is a loving one. It was just that I saw a pattern of behaviour for which I wanted to take responsibility for the first time in my life rather than continuing to excuse it. I could see that mental illness explained some of my vulnerabilities in this area, but I recognised the actual behaviours as sinful and un-Christlike, and I wanted to eliminate them as best I could.

I prayed for help with this. I also tried to cultivate an awareness of what was happening when tense situations arose, and to remind myself in the moment that mental illness did not give me licence to act out. I told Rob I wanted to change and that, from then on, if I did slip up I wasn't going to justify my behaviour based on my illness. I would take responsibility as an adult and as a Christian.

It's been a journey, and I realised I needed to develop new skills to help me manage my emotions at times of weakness. It took me some time to find the right strategies and tools (more of this in chapter 6) but even without these, the simple act of committing to take responsibility had an impact on what I said and did during moments of tension. I am gradually learning to let go of my need to be right, and to be more skilful in negotiating conflict situations. And I am consciously relating to Rob as an adult, Christian wife, not just someone with mental illness for whom he is a carer.

The other aspect of taking responsibility and acting as an adult Christian, even in times of mental distress, related to my interactions with health professionals. For years I had tended to present to my nurses as childlike and helpless. Just as I came to God with lists of things for him to fix, I came to my mental health team with lists of things I wanted them to fix for me. I am quite sure it wasn't obvious to them that I had a strengthening faith, even though they knew I was a Christian. I was not a good witness in that sense, perhaps.

I set about changing this too. It was as simple as gathering myself before appointments; adopting an upright posture and a calm, adult voice; and beginning conversations with what was going well (including the strength I was drawing from my faith) rather than with my worries and what I felt needed to change. I went a step further and tried to meet them with my suggestions of what I was going to do to bring about change rather than expecting them to come up with all the solutions.

This was an area in which I experienced an immediate improvement. I felt as though our appointments had been transformed into adult-to-adult conversations with no sense of power imbalance. I found myself talking openly about my faith, and I also felt more helped by the nurses' supportive reinforcement of my efforts to help myself than I ever had by demanding their solutions.

Encouraging people with mental illness to take responsibility for their own recovery is a key principle in the recovery model, and I was beginning to see why. The more I took responsibility for my behaviour, the greater my sense of ownership over my recovery and my wellbeing became. I felt more in control as I grew in self-control; more empowered as I drew on my own strengths. I also felt more at peace with God – the holy, pure and righteous One, and a better ambassador for him.

Committing to stay in church

Olivia had become frustrated with me in the past for running away from courses and jobs. I had addressed that, but there was another area in which I had shown a lack of commitment and perseverance. This was my church life and, alongside that, my involvement in my local community.

When I first became depressed in 2006, I was a member of a flourishing Baptist church where I had been happily settled for a few years. I wrote about my own baptism there in *Wrestling with My Thoughts*. I remained a member of this church for several years, but I was uncommitted. I dropped out of the praise group, stopped going to home groups and prayer meetings, and often attended other churches on Sundays. This was in spite of a core group of individuals within this church who never wavered in their commitment to me; indeed, to this day, some of these Christians still keep in touch with me and pray for my little family. But I am afraid that I was sometimes more affected by the few voices of those who were frustrated with me for various reasons, or who seemed to exclude me, than by the many voices of loyal friends. I felt misunderstood at times, that I could not let my guard down in church, and that I had been written off in a setting where, prior to 2006, I had contributed in many areas.

Eventually, I had decided to resign from membership, making a mistaken, mania-driven decision to write to every member expressing my disgruntlement. This is one of my greatest regrets in life. I would have left in due course anyway because of my move away from Belfast when Rob and I got married, and could have done so gracefully and gratefully. It is testimony to the great forbearance of the core membership of this church that I have been forgiven and have since been warmly welcomed when we have visited as a family.

I made more errors in dealing with another Belfast church – this time a charismatic group I often attended with a friend when I was feeling unhappy at the Baptist fellowship. It was not an ideal setting for someone suffering from psychotic episodes, as they were too easily interpreted as evidence of demonic activity, which led to a damaging encounter with 'deliverance' ministry.

However, my regrets relate more to my hot-and-cold behaviour there, sometimes trying to fling myself into getting involved in their social projects, then withdrawing without warning; sometimes getting offended when I felt I was unwelcome on certain programmes, when the reality was that the pastoral team were concerned about my mental stability; vacillating between wanting to move into membership and wanting to leave altogether – as, after a year or so, I did.

There were, of course, a few individuals who remained steady in their acceptance of me despite my broken, confused state, and again I have some contact with them today, for which I am thankful. But the end result was that, by the time I left Belfast, I had no formal ties with any church, and I felt nervous about getting involved in another.

My first few years at Rob's Presbyterian church were not easy either. I joined formally when we were married in 2015, and at this time I was not enjoying good mental health. Being, on my better days, a social person, I would often have a good conversation with someone one week and think I was on my way to making a friend. The next week, I could be feeling paranoid and unable to look the same person in the eye. If this was difficult for me, it was impossible for the other person to understand.

I tried to find a way into church life, and again made sad mistakes. I joined the choir, then, after a panic attack during a rehearsal night, I left without any explanation. I was asked if I would like to sing in one of the praise groups, and agreed (even though one of my new medications was drying my throat and my vocal performance was patchy at best). I then messed up terribly by writing an email complaining about how terrible we sounded compared to another, longer-established, group in the church, and outlining changes I felt were necessary. I never sang with them again.

Then the awful cycle of hospital admissions and discharges began, and I felt even less well understood. I became aware of local gossip – some of it inaccurate – and felt hurt and upset. As in previous congregations, there were a few kind individuals who kept in touch, visiting me and helping Rob out with meals, but I started to feel detached from the church. I don't think I ever told Rob I wanted to leave, and I didn't know where else I would go, but I definitely entertained the idea of a fresh start somewhere new in my own mind.

Beginning my recovery journey changed all of that. I began to look at all the positives of the church. I liked the teaching and the music, and I had finally made a few friends I respected and trusted. What's more, the way the Presbyterian Church functions more broadly seemed a good fit for someone with severe mental illness, with its regular rhythms, clear structure and predictable patterns. It was also local, which became important. I decided that, once and for all, I would commit to this imperfect but Christ-centred congregation . . . for the long haul.

In the recovery model, all of a person's relationships are important – not just with friends and family, but with people in local groups . . . including churches. Mental health professionals help patients build on these relationships, with the long-term aim that professional supports are eventually withdrawn. I realised I had sabotaged some important relationships with church supports more than once, making it impossible to build on them for recovery. I determined not to do this again.

My central complaint with previous churches had been: 'They don't understand me and my needs!' I decided I was no longer going to expect understanding from my church family; instead, I was going to take responsibility for helping them to understand, whatever it took.

In the end, it really helped that I had written *Wrestling with My Thoughts*. Even before the book was launched, people knew it was in the pipeline, and I was asked to share my story at the church's

Presbyterian Women event. I was overwhelmed by the response. So many ladies I had barely spoken to before came to me afterwards and thanked me for my openness and honesty.

When the book came out, I was asked to speak in the main church service, and was invited to bring copies with me. I sold about forty and had to take a few orders for more. I couldn't believe the interest. And then I began to get responses. The most common was simply: 'Thank you for helping me understand,' often followed by the more surprising, 'It takes away the fear.'

I knew that lack of understanding had been a barrier, but I hadn't realised how much it had led to fear. When I delved a bit deeper, it became apparent that people often think of horrible crimes when they hear about severe mental illness. They didn't know what it would be like to have a conversation with someone who has a severe mental illness, and were afraid of feeling uncomfortable or just saying the wrong thing.

I realised as I spoke to these warm, kind – and now accepting – people that the stigma I had felt was real, but that it had been driven by a lack of understanding, itself driven by fear. Many readers of my book have since contacted me to say that they no longer attend church because of stigma. It makes me so sad, and more determined than ever to do what I can to increase under-standing, tackling the very root of the stigma. I no longer felt I needed to run, because I was understood, and that meant I could build on many supportive relationships for my recovery.

When Rob and I had our son, we were so thankful to have committed to our church, because its members more than proved their commitment to us. We had spiritual, emotional and prac-tical support of every kind imaginable from people who knew that the birth of a baby brings challenges – not least when the mum has a history of mental illness – and wanted to walk along-side us. Reflecting back now, I don't think we could have done it without them. My recovery was in part dependent on those relationships.

Committing to stay in the community

As well as having felt unsettled in church, I had also been unsure that I wanted to stay in my local community. I can remember talking to my counsellor, Debbie, at length about how much I missed the buzz and cultural life of Belfast, and how I really didn't feel connected or rooted in the seaside resort where we now lived. I sometimes fantasised about what it would be like to move back. More than once, I looked at property websites for something affordable near my old apartment.

Once I had committed to recovery and to my church, this changed. I knew that our family life would centre around church, so I wanted to put down stronger roots in the local community. I began to build on all the things I liked about our town (investing in the positives is another principle of recovery), from the seaside and the mountains to the coffee shops and library.

I decided to involve myself more in community life. I chose one café I liked, and decided it would be my 'local', where I would go regularly and get to know the staff. I started conversations with the librarians and got to know their names. I started making donations to a local foodbank. Of course, this all came to a temporary halt with lockdown, but the foundations were in place for family life in the community – which would involve a lot of local parent-and-toddler activities later on!

A new beginning

I approached my due date in a deeper relationship with God, having identified areas of my own character I could work on, and committed to my local church and town. I had also committed to devoting my life to the two things I valued most: family and writing.

The sense of peace and inner serenity this engendered was profound. I had never felt so centred and grounded before, even in the days when I was a happy medical student and life had seemed quite simple. There was also, of course, great excitement and anticipation as Rob and I prepared to meet our son.

When my obstetrician decided to induce labour shortly after thirty-seven weeks, we felt ready. My mental state was good; my health professionals could see my determination to progress in recovery; and we knew that God already loved our little baby even more than we did (though that hardly seemed possible). On 3 July 2020, at 2.04 pm, he made his entry into the world and our lives changed for ever!

* * *

There is no sound at first. I can see that people are working with him on a resuscitation trolley. I panic.

'What's happening?' I shout.

Then it comes: his cry, growing stronger with each breath.

A midwife approaches my bed and hands him to me, a tiny bundle, creased little face first. I know I will never forget this moment. I feel my tired eyes brim with tears, my mouth break into the widest smile I've ever worn.

'Hello, baby,' I whisper, snuggling him into my chest.

He is warm and tense, fists clenched, but quickly relaxes, skin-to-skin contact helping him to settle. I look for Rob and see him standing close, leaning in to see our little boy.

'He's perfect,' I say as our eyes meet.

We laugh and clasp hands.

The three of us enjoy a short moment of closeness, while midwives gathering to my right keep a check on my blood pressure and work at my drip. One of them explains she will clean baby up a little and let his daddy hold him while the doctor works with me. We nod.

I seem to lose a minute or two to exhaustion and drugs and pain, but snap back to reality as the doctor finishes up. I look over to the soft chair near the window and see Rob there holding our blanketed parcel with a blue knitted hat on. Baby is content and Rob is beaming.

A midwife asks me whether I would be happy for Rob to give baby his first bottle while I get freshened up. I say yes, and barely take my eyes off them even as the midwives help me wash and change my nightie.

When Rob hands baby back to me, I well up again with a love that is different from any I have known. He cries and I instinctively start to sing to him, bringing his head under my chin. When he quietens, it is my turn to offer the feed.

All the staff take turns to congratulate us, calling us Mummy and Daddy. It feels as though I have been preparing for this moment all my life.

'Thank you, God,' I pray silently, 'that this little one is safely here at last!'

Dr Ken Yeow

The recovery model values 'spirituality'. How can the Church appreciate this as it seeks to serve others?

Within healthcare settings, including in the field of mental health, there is a growing recognition of the importance of spirituality in terms of potentially promoting health and wellbeing. In this context, spirituality is defined more broadly than any particular religion, and incorporates a person's identity, meaning, purpose and values. It can also refer to a belief in a 'higher power' who/which can become an object of deference as well as a source of truth and power in an individual's journey through life.

This does not mean there is widespread acceptance of the supernatural within the health sciences. Nevertheless, there is perhaps a growing openness to the reality that people are often deeply affected and influenced by things which do not seem to fit within a purely biological or naturalistic view of the world. Some things that really matter to people – relationships, love, fulfilment, joy, beauty, the innate sense that there is something more than meets the eye in this intricate and fascinating world of ours – are not easily explained and categorised scientifically.

The Church can play a part in providing a cohesive framework for a person's spirituality; one that is rooted in the grand narrative of God's redemption of broken people who live in a fallen world, but who have a real hope of better things. A Christian worldview can provide coherent and profound identity, meaning, purpose and values based on the fact that we are made in God's image and have the privilege of joining him in his work of transforming our world into one that reflects his glory. Christian community has the potential to provide the supportive connectedness human beings yearn for, binding people together through a common message of grace; one that has been faithfully handed down through countless generations of believers.

Scripture and reflection

No light matter (Psalm 139)

When I was at a Christian eating disorder treatment centre in 2008, the words of Psalm 139:13–16 were everywhere: 'You created my inmost being . . . I praise you because I am fearfully and wonderfully made . . . My frame was not hidden from you when I was made in the secret place . . . Your eyes saw my unformed body.' The idea was that young Christian women who struggled with body image could look at their bodies differently in light of these scriptures.

In *Wrestling with My Thoughts*, I described how another section of the same psalm (below) stood out for me. I realised God had been everywhere with me – in my mania, in my depression, in my psychosis – holding me in his hand.

Where can I go from your Spirit?
    Where can I flee from your presence?
If I go up to the heavens, you are there;
    if I make my bed in the depths, you are there.
If I rise on the wings of the dawn,
    if I settle on the far side of the sea,
even there your hand will guide me,
    your right hand will hold me fast.
(Psalm 139:7–10)

At the stage in my recovery where I was re-evaluating God's character and re-examining my own, verses 11–12 and 23–24 leapt from the page:

If I say, 'Surely the darkness will hide me
and the light become night around me,'
even the darkness will not be dark to you;
   the night will shine like the day,
   for darkness is as light to you . . .

Search me, God, and know my heart;
test me and know my anxious thoughts.
See if there is any offensive way in me,
and lead me in the way everlasting.

I remember reading verses 23–24 and making them a prayer: 'Search me, know me, test me . . . see if there is any offensive way in me.' I really wanted to be right with God, and for him to lead me in his way.

But reading the note on these verses in the NIV Study Bible (Zondervan, 1985) caused me to take stock for a second: 'It is no light matter to be examined by God.'[4] I thought about the awesomeness of the God I had encountered as I reread the Old Testament, of his purity, holiness, righteousness, perfectness – indeed, of how darkness is light to him (139:11–12). And of the frailties and sinfulness I had encountered as I looked inward at myself.

It is no light matter indeed, yet as I looked at the psalm again, I noticed something I had not picked up on first reading. David begins the psalm with the very words: 'You have searched me, LORD, and you know me.' I realised that God *has* examined me.

You see, when I make those verses my prayer, I am really only putting myself in a right attitude towards him, welcoming the examination that God has no need to do because he already knows me intimately . . . and has done since I was 'made in the secret place' (verse 15).

Today I read Psalm 139 in its entirety, taking each section in context, and making it all my prayer. The God who knows me . . . is the God who holds me in his right hand . . . is the God who created me . . . is the God I ask to search me. A perfect being, yet One who looks on my imperfections with grace and compassion; a perfect guide in recovery: 'Lead me in the way everlasting!' (verse 24).

Questions for personal reflection or discussion

1. How do you perceive God the Father? Have you ever doubted the rightness of his ways?
2. Have you noticed any patterns in your life that have had a negative impact on your recovery (from mental illness, another difficulty in life, or simply your flaws or sinfulness)? How might you begin to make positive change?

5
Fresh shoots

The Wellness Recovery Action Plan (WRAP)

'Learn the unforced rhythms of grace.'
(Matthew 11:28–30, MSG)

Recovery principle 7
'Individuals have a personal responsibility for their own self-
care and journeys of recovery.'

'Recovery is about changing our lives, not changing our
biochemistry.'[1]
(Pat Deegan PhD)

A new arrival and a new framework

When we took our little boy home from hospital in July 2020, I
was in a good place mentally, emotionally and spiritually. I had
been living in recovery for well over a year and, though this doesn't
seem like a long time now, it had been sustained and solid enough
that I had confidence it would continue. I had a good medication
regimen, I'd had a year of constructive talking therapy, and I was
enjoying an exciting period of growth in my relationship with
God.

Now, more than ever, with this tiny baby snuggling into my
chest, I knew I had to be completely and utterly committed to my
ongoing recovery. I was doing well, and I wanted to keep doing
well. I knew it was likely there would be blips from time to time

– one of the distinctive features of mental health recovery is that it is non-linear – but I wanted to manage these as well as possible. Rob and I were getting to know our son, and we wanted him to have a mother who could be consistently there for him and emotionally available.

I had a good foundation to build on, but I needed some kind of framework to strengthen my recovery on a day-to-day basis. It is impossible to build a rigid routine with a newborn, but I wanted to create flexible patterns of living that would support me in sustaining my good health as far as possible. I began to think through various strategies I had been given in the past for improving daily structure, and the one I decided to revisit was quite simple: the Wellness Recovery Action Plan (WRAP).

During my pregnancy, I had realised something very profound: that stress responses aren't changed by having rescue strategies (or rescue medications) to use in times of crisis. These can only de-escalate the response once it has occurred. But ongoing commitment to certain activities does lead to beneficial changes in stress responses by lowering the baseline reactivity of the nervous system. This means there is reduced sensitivity to stressors and there are smaller spikes (of fear, anxiety, irritability or anger, for example) when reactions do occur.

I was pretty sure that I had discovered some of these activities, and I wanted to build them into my life on a regular basis.

Flashback to 2016, at home

I sit on the dining room floor, back against the wall, hugging my knees. I wipe tears from my face with the back of my right hand, pursing my lips and exhaling slowly, before breaking down into sobs once more.

Rob hands me another tissue. I blow my nose, then add it to the growing sodden pile to my left.

'Help me.' My voice is thin, yet laden with urgency. 'Please!'

'I don't know what to do. You're seeing the doctor tomorrow. Let's just get through until then.'

I bite my lip and it bleeds. My words come out in stops and starts.
'I . . . can't cope . . . until . . . then.'
'Is there anyone who can help us? What about calling Olivia?'
I choke on my own tears and start to hiccup.
'Do you want me to call her?' *Rob bends towards me.*
'No,' *I sniff.* 'I can do it. What time is it in Los Angeles? 6 am? She'll be up.'
I pull my sleeve over my wrist and wipe my damp smartphone with the heel of my hand, then brush streaks of hair from my face.
'Hello?' *Olivia's voice is muffled.*
'Ol-i-via,' *I force her name out, my body shuddering with emotion.*
'What is it, Sharon?'
'I can't cope . . . any more.'
'Sorry, I'm on my way out to work. Hang on 'til I get you on the Bluetooth.'
I hear keys rattle, a car door slam.
'Okay, what's going on?'
'I'm so low . . . I can't – huh – do this . . . any more. I can't – huhuh – cope. I can't. I need help. Help me!'
'Sharon, Sharon, stop crying for a second.' *Olivia's voice is firm but kind.*
'I can't . . . cope!'
'Can't you use your tools?'
'Wh-what do you mean, tools?' *I feel my cheeks flush red.*
Olivia's tone sharpens. 'Whatever strategies the mental health people have given you for when you feel like this!'
'But I don't have any tools!'
Olivia sighs.
I gather myself a little. 'CBT doesn't work for me – I've told you that . . . I-I think my way round it. I don't know – huhuh – what else I can do . . . Please help me.'
'I wish you could see a psychologist.'
'I did, and we just talked about my childhood! And that other one just told me to "feel my feet on the ground" or something, and it's no good. Please, please help me. What am I going to do?'
'Have you taken a lorazepam?'
I blow my nose again. 'Yes. Rob gave me one about five minutes ago.'

'Well, that should be starting to work. Rob's staying with you, right?'
Rob is listening in. He puts his hand on my shoulder and nods.
'Yes,' I sigh.
'Well, just hang in there, sweetie. You're talking to the doctor tomorrow. Can you get out for a walk, and then get some rest?'
I start to feel floaty, a little calmer. The lorazepam is kicking in and there's something about talking to my aunt that usually helps me settle. I take a ragged breath in and whisper, 'Okay.'

✳ ✳ ✳

By the summer of 2020, I had come far since this snapshot of life in 2016, but I was still some way from having the kind of tools Olivia was talking about (that would come in 2021 – see chapter 6); however, I thought developing a WRAP might be one tool I could use to implement some activities that would help to sustain my positive mental state.

I had first encountered WRAP during my first year of engagement with the recovery college, though I had been admitted to hospital by the time the relevant course came around. I did make one back then with the help of an inpatient occupational therapist, but at that time I lacked a recovery mindset. The document I produced was heavy with lists of stressors, triggers and early warning signs, and light on actions to take when they occurred.

I found my old WRAP again in 2020, but decided to start from scratch. Attending a course would have been difficult with a baby, but I discovered there was now a free WRAP app. I downloaded this and, during baby's naptimes, set to work.

What is a WRAP?[2]

A Wellness Recovery Action Plan (WRAP) is described by its creators as 'a simple and powerful process for creating the life and wellness you want'.

WRAP was born out of the movement for mental health recovery in the US during the 1990s. Led by Mary Ellen Copeland, a researcher and peer support group facilitator who had herself suffered serious mental illness, a group of 'survivors' of mental illness came together to discuss practical strategies for regaining and sustaining their own wellness. The WRAP was developed as a system anyone could use to organise these strategies for their own recovery.

WRAP is now used in at least fifteen countries, including through the NHS in the UK, and has been adapted for many different life issues as well as mental health recovery. In 2010, after being shown to improve symptoms of mental illness and promote recovery, hopefulness, self-advocacy and improved quality of life, WRAP was designated as an evidence-based practice by the body which oversees mental healthcare in the US (SAMSHA).

A WRAP is built around a 'wellness toolbox': 'a list of skills and strategies for keeping us well and for feeling better if we don't feel well'. These wellness tools (which could be anything from taking a brisk walk to phoning a particular friend, from reading the Bible to spending ten minutes meditating – all of which are on my list) are the foundation for each of the six parts of the WRAP:

1. Daily plan: what wellness looks like for us and what we need to do every day to stay well.
2. Stressors: events or situations that may disrupt wellness, and the tools to prevent this.
3. Early warning signs: indicators that we need to use tools to protect or restore our wellness.
4. Signs that things are breaking down or getting much worse: and actions to prevent crisis.
5. Crisis plan: a directive to help us maintain control, including what we want others to do.
6. Post-crisis plan: how we want to navigate back to the daily plan, perhaps with added tools.

WRAP has only been proven to be effective when developed within a peer group setting where trained peer co-facilitators meet with participants for two hours weekly for eight to twelve weeks. However, WRAP materials are available to anyone to use independently or with whatever support they want.

I have found the WRAP app simple and straightforward to use, and it allows me to email a PDF of my WRAP to anyone I feel should be aware of my plan (should a crisis ever arise, for example).

Rhythms of living

I shared my WRAP with a few key people in my life so that they could support me (and would know my wishes should a crisis occur), and committed to updating it as I made progress in recovery. I would find new items to add to my wellness toolbox or adjust my daily plan as my routine adapted with changes in baby's needs and routine.

Since my WRAP needs to remain a living document, I reviewed it prior to writing this chapter, and could see that I had been neglecting a couple of items I had recorded as 'things I need to do to stay well'. This very day, as I sit down to write, I have been going through a downturn in my mood, and I realise that if I didn't have a WRAP I might not have identified these omissions as possible contributing factors. Today, I can say that I have re-implemented daily outdoor exercise and a brief morning meditation session to help me towards regaining my wellbeing.

From my earliest experiences of mental healthcare, I have seen that professionals believe structure and routine, with daily and weekly rhythms, to be key to psychological and emotional wellbeing. WRAP builds on this, creating a flexible daily routine with preordained changes to make when early signs of deteriorating mental health are recognised. The flexibility is vital for a creative person like me – especially with a small child in the house – but even creatives achieve more when they have a basic structure.

As I have studied the Bible, and particularly as I reread it in its entirety during my pregnancy, I have been reminded that God instituted rhythms of life from the very beginning. Our seven-day week with its day of rest was instituted at the point of creation itself. We also have biblical provision for daily routines. I think of Psalm 92, which begins: 'It is good to praise the LORD and make music to your name, O Most High, proclaiming your love in the morning and your faithfulness at night.'

God created summer and winter, seedtime and harvest; times to fast and times to feast; years to farm and years to let the land lie fallow. The maker of the stars and planets understood that rhythms of living – structure and routine – are good for his creation. I found this to be true as I constructed my WRAP and recognised the things I need to do each day to stay well.

As a Christian, these included a time of prayer and reading the Bible. I also included my need to take time for deeper theological study (the benefits of which I had discovered while I was pregnant), but I found that as I used the WRAP I needed to revise this, as life with a little one simply didn't allow me the space or mental capacity. I expect I will be able to re-evaluate in the future and there will be a place for study again.

It was the daily plan that I found most helpful in summer 2020 when our baby was born. I had lived in recovery for long enough to know the kinds of things that helped me to stay well, and now that I had a child who needed me, I was determined to work around his routine to fit these in.

On the other hand, I found that the wellness tools I had identified – particularly those I would implement if I began to experience stressors or notice early warning signs – were blunt instruments. I knew that taking a hot shower with a favourite scented shower gel was a healthy and nourishing thing for me to do, but it would probably help anyone to some degree, and was not specific to a particular symptom or need I might have. What's more, as with other tools in my box, it was not necessarily easy to do while I had responsibility for a baby. I needed it as part of my daily plan, but it was not going to relieve a sudden moment of anxiety in the afternoon.

Sharper wellness tools were to come later in the year, and particularly early in 2021 (as I will explain in chapter 6). However, in the process of working with my WRAP and reading around the kinds of things that seemed to be helpful for me, I made a startling discovery about my recovery process.

I had noticed during my pregnancy, and now as I moved into motherhood, that I seemed to be less reactive in stressful situations than I had been previously. I had assumed this was due to my new medication regimen – and I'm sure this was helping – but I began to read about the part of the brain that regulates the body's stress response: the amygdala.

I learned that certain daily practices – particularly mindfulness, including mindful yoga – can reduce the size of the amygdala and 'downregulate' its activity; that is, reduce its response during stress.

A definition of mindfulness

Jon Kabat-Zinn, a psychological researcher and the founder of Mindfulness-Based Stress Reduction, defines mindfulness as: 'The awareness that arises through paying attention, on purpose, in the present moment, non-judgmentally.'[3]

Some Christians feel uneasy about mindfulness, knowing that some forms of mindfulness originated from Eastern religion. But when we dissociate the practice from its origins and define it as Jon does, I believe mindfulness is consistent with Christian faith. Sometimes the term 'secular mindfulness' is used by psychologists who teach the practice to make it clear that there is no religious content. When using online mindfulness resources, I find this a useful search term.

Mindfulness can involve sitting quietly and focusing on your breathing for a few minutes; a short exercise such as paying attention to the sensations in your feet on the floor (similar to what the psychologist tried to teach me back in 2016); or simply becoming more aware of all that is around you: the colours of the flowers as you walk outside or the aroma of fresh coffee.

I first encountered this kind of practice through yoga, but later began practising secular mindful meditation, something I will write more about in chapter 6. I also developed a more mindful approach to everyday life – using all my senses to become more aware in every present moment.

As I see it, paying attention to each moment is biblical. In his Sermon on the Mount, Jesus taught us to live in the present, saying: 'Therefore do not worry about tomorrow, for tomorrow will worry about itself. Each day has enough trouble of its own' (Matthew 6:34).

I can see in my own life how cultivating a simple awareness of what is happening right now, rather than mulling over the past or planning for (and worrying about) the future, has made me more like Jesus. I am more available to the people around me, less preoccupied with how other people perceive me, and freer to notice the wonders of creation around me and to respond in worship.

What is the amygdala?[4]

There are two linked amygdalae – small, almond-shaped clusters of cells – located deep within the brain's temporal lobes. The amygdala is part of the limbic system (involved in processing emotion and memory), and is the seat of the brain's primal fight-or-flight response.

If the amygdala senses a threat, it triggers the release of stress hormones in a split second, increasing the heartrate and priming the body for action. This occurs before the prefrontal cortex (associated with awareness, concentration and decision-making) can process the perceived threat, often identifying that there is no real danger.

Using MRI scanning, it has been shown that an eight-week course of mindfulness meditation causes the amygdala to shrink and the prefrontal cortex to thicken. What's more, connections between the amygdala and the remainder of the brain weaken, while connections between areas associated with attention and concentration get stronger. In other words, the amygdala is less responsive, enabling a more thoughtful approach to emotional stimuli.

As a Christian, I see this adaptation of the amygdala as something worth pursuing, as it allows for increased self-control – one of the fruits of the Spirit (Galatians 5:22–23).

Yoga and the amygdala

As it happened, short sessions of yoga in the morning and evening had been part of my routine for some time. I had tried yoga when I was at medical school, but had given it up after having doubts about whether it was a suitable activity for Christians. I was aware that it had roots in Eastern philosophies and wondered whether it, too, was some other form of religion.

I was surprised to find that it was part of the curriculum at New Beginnings, a Christian treatment centre where I spent time in 2008. Here it was seen as a gentle form of exercise that was unlikely to become an obsessive behaviour for eating disorder patients (the programme used burned few calories). It was also a generally calming and nourishing activity during days that were busy with challenging therapy sessions.

A note on rejecting the spiritual associations of yoga

Like mindfulness, yoga has been associated with Eastern religions; most frequently, Hinduism and Buddhism. However, it is a myth that yoga in itself is a religion. The Sanskrit word for yoga is, simply translated, 'union', and this is frequently used to refer to the mindful union of body and breath (so I breathe in as I move my body into one position and breathe out as I move back to my original position).

The Collins English Dictionary first defines yoga as 'a type of exercise in which you move your body into various positions in order to become more fit or flexible, to improve your breathing, and to relax your mind'.[5] This definition detaches yoga from any spiritual origins, and it is with this in mind that I practise yoga, and that I write of yoga in this book. Yoga has indeed helped me to become fitter and more flexible, improved my breathing and relaxed my mind.

Of course, it is possible to research the spiritual associations of yoga and find that there are philosophies of yoga that would be of concern to Christians. I firmly reject any yoga teaching that promotes Hinduism or Buddhism, and have found it possible to practise yoga daily for the past fourteen years without evoking any spiritual aspect of yoga philosophy. I simply choose my teachers by the secular values they espouse and choose practices that embody a union of body and breath, promoting physical and mental wellbeing.

In all this time, my faith has remained strong, I have felt no temptation to investigate the philosophies of yoga further, and I believe that I have reaped great benefits – which have helped me to become more Christlike. I think it is important to be discerning, but also to remember that God has dispensed common grace to all people, and we can derive benefit from sources that are not explicitly Christian.

It is worth mentioning that there is an established organisation called the Christian Yoga Association, and there are several schools that offer yoga teacher training with a Christian worldview. In North America, in particular, many people simply think of yoga as another form of physical and mental exercise, grouping it with Pilates classes and similar. It was in this context that yoga was used at New Beginnings, positioned in the programme alongside aerobics and stretch class.

I practise yoga on my own at home because it suits me to do so, but it also allows me to retain more control over the content of my practices. I used to attend classes in person, but found that my local teacher was interested in Buddhism and incorporated aspects of its philosophy. Since I reject this as contrary to my faith, I prefer to use online videos with secular content only.

When I returned home from the US, I bought a DVD of two beginners' yoga practices led by the secular teacher whose programme had been used at New Beginnings. I began to spend forty-five minutes every evening developing a basic yoga routine. Again, I found it calming, and that my breathing remained calmer and steadier afterwards, and my body became stronger and more flexible. Even my mother, who is a physiotherapist, commented that my posture had never been so good, which in turn helped with the back pain I had experienced since my student days.

Yoga has been a part of my life ever since. In 2017, I discovered a YouTube channel, Yoga With Adriene, with hundreds of secular yoga videos. I later joined her app for an ad-free experience with even more videos. At home, and especially during hospital admissions – during which I always had my mat with me – I learned to choose appropriate videos for when I felt sad or anxious, depressed or agitated. Over time I found that, regardless of the state I was in when I sat down on the mat, I always got up twenty or thirty minutes later feeling calmer and more in control.

What I didn't realise was that, doing this twice each day, on average, I was downregulating my amygdala and reducing my baseline reactivity to stress rather than just feeling the benefits in the immediate aftermath of my practice. When I began to learn about the amygdala, I realised I had probably had a particularly large and well-developed one! By this point, those flashpoints during my day – a disagreement with Rob, a difficult appointment, a worry about our son – didn't produce such heightened emotions . . . and other people were beginning to recognise that in me too.

It wasn't just tools for crises I needed, though these were invaluable when they came. I needed to change my way of being, my lifestyle, in order to reduce the frequency of crisis moments, manage my anxiety and develop better means of self-soothing.

As I began to realise that yoga was only one means of living more mindfully, I decided to add mindfulness practices to the section in my WRAP where there is room for 'wellness tools I would like to develop'. I went on a Zoom mindfulness course through the recovery college, learned more about research which showed that secular mindfulness meditation changes the anatomy of the brain, and became convinced that I needed to live more mindfully moment to moment, not just during specific times of meditation.

Of course, you might well decide that yoga is not for you, either because you don't enjoy it, or because of other concerns. There are many other activities that might focus your mind while improving your physical fitness and generating healing endorphins. I have one friend with mental illness who hits the gym twice a day for a serious workout, another who runs outdoors a few times a week. It may be that an alternative class –Pilates, perhaps – suits you better.

The important thing in terms of addressing overactivation of the amygdala is that the physical exercise is mindful and incorporates mindfulness of the breath. Most of us do not breathe deeply enough in our day-to-day lives, often due to stress and anxiety, and this promotes a vicious cycle of increasing stress and anxiety, and an increasingly shallow breathing pattern. Regular mindful exercise can break this cycle, and certainly has done in my experience.

DBT: a therapy worth pursuing

There was another important item I decided to add to my 'wellness tools I would like to develop'. I recalled a conversation I'd had with a nurse one day while I was an inpatient back in 2017. He watched me pack up my yoga mat and then observed that I should investigate dialectical behavioural therapy (DBT).

I was quite taken aback because I knew that DBT had been developed for a condition called borderline personality disorder (BPD, also known as emotionally unstable personality disorder), an illness defined by the inability to regulate emotions, resulting in drastic mood swings even within the space of a day, and for people with chronic suicidal thoughts. In the past, patients with BPD were considered 'difficult', hard to treat – even manipulative, though thankfully nowadays professionals approach them with more compassion.

I thought at the time that my nurse was implying I had BPD rather than schizoaffective disorder, but looking back I realise this was not his intention at all; he had simply observed that I found yoga helpful enough to be committed to practising it daily, and knew that there was some crossover between mindful yoga and the kind of skills taught in DBT, so I might find its approach suited me.

Although I shied away from investigating DBT at that time, a seed had been planted. In 2020, as I sought to make my WRAP more personalised and effective, I decided to read more about it.

DBT was invented and developed by an eminent American psychologist called Dr Marsha M. Linehan. She made the news in 2020 by publishing a memoir in which she confessed that she had developed DBT from her own personal experience. It was previously little known that she had been chronically suicidal as a young woman and had spent time in inpatient psychiatric care.

I read her autobiography, *Building a Life Worth Living* (Random House, 2020), and was fascinated by Marsha's journey and the way she had taken ownership of her situation and done everything she could to get out of her 'emotional hell', vowing to help others get out too. In time, she became a psychologist and researcher, and the DBT she developed is now the gold standard treatment for BPD and suicidality worldwide. It is also used for depression and eating disorders. In chapter 6, I will explain how exploring DBT finally gave me personal and effective wellness tools with which to extend my WRAP.

With WRAP, I learned more about taking personal responsibility for my own mental health and how to advocate for myself, including how to explain what works for me and what doesn't in appointments with mental health professionals.

With this process came a sharp lesson in humility. For years I had almost taken pride in the fact that my illness was so severe, simple things wouldn't work for me. When nurses made suggestions of things that might help on a bad day, I would knock them down, one after another, as pointless and ineffective for me, while acknowledging that they might be good for other people.

There had also been an element of fear. What would happen to me if they did work and I lost the support I had come to rely on so much? I am thankful for the many supports I had during my difficult years, but I can see that, at some point, they became an impediment to my recovery because I valued them more than health itself. Of course, supports don't just suddenly drop away when there is slight improvement, but it was hard for me to believe that at the time.

Small changes, significant impact

Once I recognised I was not so special, I had to try the things that worked for other people because there were good reasons why they were recommended. I became willing to give them a genuine trial, rather than a half-hearted one, and found that they often made a difference . . . even if it was small.

I began to realise that small things add up to significant change, and I was so committed to recovery that I was willing to do ten extra things in a day if together they would generate improvement. By now, as a new mum, it was much more valuable to me to be well than to have support, and simple things such as a WRAP gave me confidence that I could survive without constant input from professionals (though at this stage, all of my professional supports remained in place, with nurses monitoring my mental health closely to ensure that I was well enough to parent).

I think of one item in particular: my SAD lamp. As a Christian, I know the significance of light. Jesus is the light of the world (John 8:12) and God's word is a 'light on my path' (Psalm 119:105). Yet for years I had rejected the possibility of using a simple UV light source – the seasonal affective disorder (SAD) lamp – to boost my mood.

Again, I thought, *I don't have SAD; I have the severest depression. That would never work for me.* In 2020 I revisited the idea, and when a friend offered to lend me her SAD lamp, I was grateful and willing to try it. I have used it for at least half an hour every day since, usually while reading or writing. It's hard to quantify its effect, but my mood is better overall than it once was, and on dark days I feel a definite boost after my light session.

My SAD lamp has become a reminder of God's call to me to walk 'out of darkness into his wonderful light' (1 Peter 2:9). It has no spiritual power, but it helps at a physical level to bring me out of the darkness of depression, and I choose to see it as a pointer to Jesus.

So I committed to using my WRAP's daily plan, staying aware of stressors and early warning signs, and implementing changes when necessary to manage blips. At first, after having our baby, the earliest sign of a drop in mood terrified me because I knew I needed to be well for him. In time, I grew in confidence because I could see that, using my WRAP, I could manage my symptoms and regain my equilibrium. Using my WRAP helped me to accept ongoing symptoms – an expected part of mental health recovery – because I no longer needed to fear them.

As I worked with my WRAP, I also committed to taking mindfulness and DBT skills from the 'tools I would like to develop' into daily life. This was my next endeavour.

Dr Ken Yeow

Can practising mindfulness be beneficial to Christians or is it too bound up in other religions?

Mindfulness is a way of 'being' that incorporates acceptance rather than judgement, observation rather than reaction, and the determination to live in a more fully engaged way in the present moment. It has its roots in ancient wisdom and Eastern religions, and has grown in popularity within the Western world, and indeed in healthcare settings where systematic research has demonstrated its possible benefits to health and wellbeing. It has understandably gained traction in the fast-paced, complex, information-saturated environment the modern world has become, where noise and distraction regularly disrupt the ability to think and reflect effectively.

In and of themselves, the principles associated with mindfulness are not anathema to the Christian faith; indeed, one could argue that they are also rooted in the contemplative Christian tradition. Acceptance and non-judgementalism, observation and reflection, and being fully present in the moment can be mirrored in the biblical practices and injunctions of being anxious for nothing, not worrying about tomorrow, being still and knowing God, and walking in the Spirit. So, in drawing out the valuable essence of its practice, there needn't be undue fear that mindfulness implies any capitulation to anti-Christian philosophies.

If anything, Christianity may well provide a way to practise a form of 'ultimate mindfulness'. By this, I mean it could supply a focus and fullness to mindfulness that might be missed in secular practice. For example, taking the time to stop and savour the smell of a rose could be enhanced by gratitude for the work of a divine Creator; the acceptance of a troublesome dilemma could be enriched by knowledge of the love of God in Christ and the promise of his sustaining presence. Rather than trying to empty the mind of active thought, God himself could become a holy preoccupation in and for the moment.

Scripture and reflection

The unforced rhythms of grace

Matthew 11:28–30:

Come to me, all you who are weary and burdened, and I will give you rest. Take my yoke upon you and learn from me, for I am gentle and humble in heart, and you will find rest for your souls. For my yoke is easy and my burden is light.

Matthew 11:28–30 (MSG):

Are you tired? Worn out? Burned out on religion? Come to me. Get away with me and you'll recover your life. I'll show you how to take a real rest. Walk with me and work with me – watch how I do it. Learn the unforced rhythms of grace. I won't lay anything heavy or ill-fitting on you. Keep company with me and you'll learn to live freely and lightly.

The rhythms I established with my WRAP felt quite forced at first. Did I really need to take that hour-long walk every day? Was it so very important to eat meals at the same times? Or to meditate for just five minutes? Many Christians schedule what they call a 'quiet time' to be alone with God, pray and reflect every day. Would it really matter, I wondered, if I dropped mine when I was sleep-deprived?

Over time, as I began to use my wellness tools to manage fluctuations in my mood and anxiety levels, it became clear that sticking to my daily plan really could make a difference to my mental health. And of course, continuing with quiet times made a difference to my spiritual health.

In Matthew 11:28–30, Jesus promises rest for all those who are 'weary and burdened', a feeling those of us with mental health problems can identify with, for his 'yoke is easy' and his 'burden is light'. I love the language used in *The Message* translation: 'Learn the unforced rhythms of grace . . . Keep company with me and you'll learn to live freely and lightly.'

If I can live my life in a way that is mindful of God's grace towards me – how he gave me salvation I did not deserve and continues his gentle daily work to make me more like Jesus – I will truly feel light and free. Mindfulness – paying attention, on purpose, in the present moment – is key here. God's grace always exists for me; I need only be aware of it . . . and then I can enjoy its unforced rhythms.

'Keeping company with Jesus' is as simple as being mindful of his presence. Lean in to this form of mindfulness today.

Questions for personal reflection or discussion

1. Do you think wellness recovery action planning is relevant even for those without diagnosed mental illnesses? How could it help your own wellbeing and spiritual health?
2. Which rhythms help you maintain your wellbeing? Are there any spiritual disciplines that you have neglected? How can you tap into the unforced rhythms of grace and find rest today?

6

Pruning

Dealing with powerful emotions

'But the fruit of the Spirit is love, joy, peace, forbearance,
kindness, goodness, faithfulness, gentleness and self-control.
Against such things there is no law.'
(Galatians 5:22–23)

Recovery principle 8
'Individuals optimize their autonomy and independence to
the greatest extent possible by leading, controlling, and exercising choice over the services and supports that assist their
recovery and resilience.'

'I made a vow to God that I would get myself out of hell and
that, once I did, I would go back into hell and get others out.
That vow has guided and controlled most of my life since
then.'[1]
(Marsha M. Linehan PhD, psychologist and research scientist)

The dining room, 5.40 pm

*Steam has stopped rising from the broccoli. The bubbly cheese on top
of the vegetable lasagne is congealing. I look at the clock. I served up
our dinner ten minutes ago and there's still no sign of Rob.*

*The front door creaks open. I hear clunky boots in the hall, then the
tap running at the bathroom sink. More minutes pass.*

*My finger taps the table. I feel heat in my neck and cheeks. My
breathing is shallow, my chest tight. I clench and unclench my fists.*

Rob sheepishly pokes his head around the dining room door. 'Sorry, I'll be with you in a second.'

How am I going to get back on schedule for bathtime and bed? What is the point in cooking nice meals if they're going to be eaten cold? Hot tears sting my eyes.

As Rob comes in, I realise something important: I am in 'emotion mind'.

Immediately, I scan my mind for the right skills to turn the situation around.

Stop! *I say to myself internally, though it sounds loud in my head.* S-T-O-P. *I freeze. I'm not going to make a move until I get my head into a better place. 'T'? Take a step back. I pull my chair away from the table and take a deep breath, hold it, then let it out slowly. 'O'? Observe! What is happening here? Rob is late. The dinner is cold. I am in emotion mind, and feeling urges to scold and lecture. Rob has apologised. 'P'? Proceed mindfully.*

I observe again for a split second. I'm mindful that my breathing is still shallow, I'm still hot and my pulse is still racing. I need to take action to regain control of my emotions. STOP has bought me a bit of time, but I need more. Which distress tolerance skill will work quickest?

Rob looks at me, one eyebrow raised.

'Excuse me for one minute,' I say, getting up from my seat.

Rob nods and we exchange the briefest of glances.

Baby, happily oblivious, is turning the pages of his book as he sits in his highchair.

In the bathroom, I plug the sink and run the cold tap. I breathe in and out slowly, making the exhalations longer than the inhalations. I move the little clock on the shelf down so I can hear its ticking. Then I breathe out, take a deep breath in, pinch my nose and plunge my face into the cold, cold water.

I start to count the seconds inside my head. One, two, three . . . twenty-eight, twenty-nine, thirty! I raise my head, gasping. I grab a towel and catch the water dripping from my chin and hair.

I take a moment to really feel the effects. My heart has slowed, my breathing has steadied. My shoulders drop and the heat drains from my neck. The dive manoeuvre has worked!

I make my way back to the dining room.

'Are you okay?' asks Rob, scratching his ear.

'I am now, thanks.'

I've bought myself more time and regained my composure. Now I need to be willing to move forward in a healthy way, with my long-term goal of maintaining good relationships and living in line with my values foremost in my mind. I open my hands and deliberately lift the corners of my mouth, communicating positive emotions and warm thoughts about Rob to my brain.

My pulse settles further.

I do a quick 'fact check'. My emotions are understandable but disproportionate. It's time to 'act opposite' to them . . .

'You've been working hard, love. I'll just put your dinner in the microwave. Do you want to take a minute or two to organise yourself before we pray?'

'Thanks,' Rob answers, putting a hand on my shoulder.

The clock now reads 5.45. I know bathtime might be a bit later tonight, but maybe we can make up a few minutes as we go. I feel a deep sense of calm in any case. We can always have a coolheaded chat about mealtimes at some calmer juncture.

As we tuck in to reheated dinners, we chat amicably. I note to myself that I am back in 'wise mind' and have a satisfying sense of mastery over my emotions. On this occasion, as on so many others, I am thankful for DBT!

Fine-tuning my emotional responses

In the last chapter, I explained how I read Marsha Linehan's memoir, which rekindled my interest in DBT. Early in 2021, with my WRAP working for me at a day-to-day level, I wanted to find out whether DBT skills might help me manage my moods on an hour-to-hour basis.

Overall, I felt as though my mental state was good, and I knew I was coping much better with parenthood than some had expected, given my history. But minor crises and dips in mood were happening from time to time, and I could see that my responses needed some fine-tuning.

DBT was developed to help people who were chronically suicidal, which meant that the biggest patient group for which it was
initially prescribed was those with a diagnosis of BPD. Patients
with BPD have great difficulty in regulating their emotions, often
experiencing dramatic mood swings several times within one
day, and the condition is associated with self-harming and other
destructive behaviours.

As I explained in chapter 5, BPD has not always elicited sym-
pathy from mental health professionals, who have not always seen
it as an illness, but, as the label suggests, a disorder of personality
itself – something very difficult to treat. Thankfully, in more recent
years, research into the causes of the condition and advances in its
treatment – including the development of DBT – have meant that
the plight of patients is better understood, and professionals no
longer need see those with BPD as untreatable.

When my nurse suggested I might be interested in DBT, I was
concerned that he, and maybe others working with him, thought I
had BPD. I'd had a formal diagnosis of schizoaffective disorder for
about seven years at this point, but I feared the addition of another,
more pejorative, label (which had once been raised as one of many
diagnostic possibilities back in 2009). As it happened, he had no
such thing in mind, but I did start to read about BPD and emotional dysregulation, and I found it interesting.

As I looked through the diagnostic criteria, I could see that I
would not meet a threshold for BPD, but I recognised that, for
between seven and fourteen days of every month, I demonstrated
some of the symptoms. My premenstrual syndrome (PMS), experienced by most women before their period, was at the severe end of
the scale. During this time, I felt my emotions strongly and found
it difficult to regulate them.

I did not self-harm (though I had done so at a very early stage in
my illness when I was taking a medication that made me agitated
and impulsive), and I was definitely not suicidal. However, I was
sometimes overwhelmed by emotions I could not even name, and
it was debilitating. I began to wonder whether DBT might help me
during these challenging weeks.

Prior to my recovery, I had put all my difficulties in regulating my emotions down to my schizoaffective disorder, believing they could only be fixed by health professionals using medications or other interventions. Now that I had begun to approach life with a recovery mindset, I was on the lookout for things I could do something about for myself. Addressing my struggle with managing powerful emotions seemed to belong in this category.

Getting to know my own body

I had been on a journey of discovery about my own body in the year since I had delivered our baby. Of course, the usual monthly hormonal cycle stops during pregnancy, and I had been on the combined oral contraceptive pill (which also eliminates hormonal cycling) for some years before this. I could no longer take the pill because my blood pressure, which had caused problems during my pregnancy, remained high after the birth. This meant it was not safe for my GP to continue prescribing it, as the pill carries a risk of stroke and so does hypertension.

In other words, during this second year of mental health recovery, I was experiencing the effects of hormonal cycling on my body for the first time in some years. Indeed, it took me several months to recognise that this was happening to me, and to identify its effects. I actually called my GP twice during the first six months of baby's life to say that I was okay but wanted him to be aware that I'd had a difficult week, just in case things got worse and I needed his help. Things did not get worse on either occasion. What did happen was that I got my period and my depression lifted.

Over time, as I began to pay more attention to my physical and emotional state in relation to my periods (and ultimately started to use a menstrual tracking app), I realised the same thing happened with every cycle. I would manage well in the first half, feeling upbeat, and that my thinking was clear and rational. During the second half my mood would drop, and I would become emotionally labile, crying easily and becoming more irritable.

I felt very embarrassed talking about this, even to my female mental health nurse, because I was conditioned by stigma around 'women's issues' and felt I should just accept PMS and get on with life. After all, every woman must deal with it, and some brands of feminism have worked very hard to prove to men that women are not volatile and unpredictable around their periods.

In time, however, as my own pattern crystallised and I began to be able to predict my moods, I started to research other women's experiences. I discovered there is a diagnosable condition called premenstrual dysphoric disorder (PMDD), where significant and debilitating depression occurs for two weeks of each cycle. A variant of this, premenstrual exacerbation (PME), is diagnosed where this deterioration in mood occurs against a background of existing mental illness. After careful checking of diagnostic criteria, and some more detailed self-monitoring, I diagnosed myself with 'PME of schizoaffective disorder'. (I told my psychiatrist only recently, and she felt this was reasonable.)

I knew I was ineligible for the combined contraceptive pill and did not think my PME was severe enough to merit additional antidepressant medication, but I felt this recognition of my cycling moods had already empowered me, as I could now predict when I was likely to get better again. I spoke briefly to my GP about it during a consultation about another problem, but decided not to seek further psychiatric help. I was happy that I was well overall, that my general medication regimen was still working, and that I could cope with the mood changes. All the same, I was intrigued to find out whether DBT would give me the tools I needed to manage the most difficult days of PME.

DBT skills training

I never seriously considered the possibility of pursuing formal DBT through my local healthcare trust. I would not have met the referral criteria, and I knew there was a waiting list of more than a year, even for those assessed as appropriate for treatment. More importantly than that, I had overall stability in my life now that I was walking in recovery, and I was not certain that enrolling in a treatment group alongside people who were very unwell would be good for me.

Instead, I wondered whether I could learn DBT skills for myself. There is a distinction between DBT and DBT skills training. DBT is usually a year-long programme involving individual psychotherapy with a DBT therapist, telephone coaching, group DBT skills training sessions and a therapist consultation team. DBT skills training is where DBT skills are taught in isolation, without individual talking therapy, coaching or team case management.

DBT is of proven effectiveness for BPD, post-traumatic stress disorder and eating disorders. DBT skills training has shown benefits for those with BPD, but also for patients with major depressive disorder, bipolar disorder and problem drinking.

Having the bipolar type of schizoaffective disorder, with a tendency towards depression, I decided to learn DBT skills in isolation. I was not likely to be able to simulate individual DBT therapy through reading books or online learning. Later, as I read more, I became a little concerned that 'dialectics' – the theory underpinning DBT – might lead me in a direction that was not consistent with my faith. This did not seem to be a problem with DBT skills training alone.

(It is worth noting here that Dr Linehan started out as a Catholic Christian and certainly values prayer, which is prominent within DBT, although the God – or god – to whom the prayer is directed is not specified. She is now a Zen Master, though she does not see this as incompatible with her continued faith in a spiritual power.)

What is 'dialectics' and how does it inform DBT?

A 'dialectic' has been defined by Oxford Languages as: 'Inquiry into metaphysical contradictions and their solutions' (I'll call this definition one) and: 'The art of investigating or discussing the truth of opinions' (definition two).[2]

These definitions may seem oblique, and at first glance I found it hard to see how they informed a behavioural talking therapy, but Dr Linehan explains that: 'As a world view or philosophical position [definition one], dialectics forms the basis of the therapeutic approach presented in this book [DBT]. Alternatively, as a form of dialogue and relationship [definition two], dialectics refers to the treatment approach or strategies used by the therapist to effect change.'[3] In other words, both definitions are relevant to the practice of DBT.

The dialectic worldview initially appeared alien to me as a Christian, leaving God out of its description of reality. In a handout for patients, Dr Linehan identifies four 'truths' of which dialectics reminds us:

1. The universe is filled with opposing sides and opposing forces (so there is always more than one way to see a situation, and two apparently opposite things can both be true).
2. Everything and every person is connected in some way.
3. Change is the only constant.
4. Change is transactional (so we influence our environment and other people, and they influence us in turn).[4]

After reading this, I became concerned about whether DBT was an appropriate therapy to pursue as a Christian. After all, I do not believe that *change* is the only constant; I believe that *God* is constant. However, I knew that New Beginnings had used DBT skills in its programme. I wondered whether there were 'common grace' benefits to be gleaned from DBT, even if I did not fully buy into the theories behind it.

Certainly, I identified with the three key dialectics Dr Linehan draws out as most relevant to her therapy:[5]

1. [The dialectic] between patients' need to accept themselves as they are in a particular moment, and the need for them to change.

This dialectic underpins the theory of mental health recovery: I need to accept where I am, with the symptoms and side effects I experience, but invest in the positives (changing what I can) to make life as worthwhile as possible.

2. [The dialectic] between getting what they need to become more competent in life, and losing what they need (for example, emotional support) if they become more competent.

I mentioned this in chapter 3, where I wrote about my own fears that getting better would cause me to lose the supports I had because of my illness.

3. [And the dialectic] between preserving their integrity and validating their own perspectives on their problems, and learning new skills that could help them to leave behind their suffering.

This final dialectic is more complex, but I think it boils down to being able to acknowledge that I have been doing the best I can – that my emotional state is not my fault, and that acquiring new skills now does not negate this or mean that I was a weak person beforehand.

It is worth mentioning that dialectics has informed the thought processes of certain theologians, notably Barth and Brunner (drawing on the ideas of Søren Kierkegaard), and that at one time there was even a journal of dialectical theology called *Between the Times*. According to Davie et al. in *New Dictionary of Theology* (IVP, 2016), dialectical theology recognises that God is so far above our understanding that we are forced to talk about him in ways that sometimes seem contradictory.

Dialectical theologians propose that the distinctions between God and humanity, eternity and time, infinite and finite, find their ultimate synthesis in Jesus Christ, in whom we also encounter both judgement and mercy. The dialectical theologians of the twentieth century ultimately recognised that some elements of dialectics are to be rejected, but generally failed to reach a consensus on what should be affirmed.

I find that dialectics is complicated to understand and to explain, and the dialectical worldview is inadequate to me as a Christian. However, I can see how its incomplete truth can still inform a useful treatment, and that viewing it through a lens of faith might even enhance its benefits.

A compassionate approach

My first thought was to read Marsha's own textbooks on DBT. I bought her seminal *DBT Skills Training Manual* (Guilford Press, 2015), which is used by all therapists practising formal DBT. I thought that it would allow me to teach myself the skills, but I quickly began to struggle, soon getting out of my depth in teaching notes designed by a psychologist for other psychologists.

I gave up before I had even reached the modules containing the individual skills. However, I was impressed by the emphasis on approaching patients with compassion (where those with BPD might previously have been dismissed or even treated with contempt). Dr Linehan emphasised that her patient group experiences such intense emotions because of biological vulnerability (they inherit these traits), and because of 'invalidating' childhood environments. This means that their early displays of emotion were not met with appropriate responses. Perhaps they were not believed or taken seriously. For example, 'I feel sad.' 'No you don't – you're perfectly fine.'

I could identify with some of Marsha's thinking, and it helped me to fully accept and acknowledge the difficulties I had pinpointed in terms of managing my own emotional responses. I developed some self-compassion and felt less of a need to downplay or explain away my most intense feelings.

My appetite for learning DBT skills to help manage these feelings had grown. I sat down one evening and Googled 'online DBT training'. One of the first links that came up was for Recovery College Online, an initiative of an English health trust to make some of its recovery college's courses accessible to anyone in the UK. Under the heading 'Communication and Behaviour' appeared the option 'DBT Skills Resource'. I wanted to know more, so I decided to enrol.

Exploring the DBT Skills Resource

It turned out that the DBT Skills Resource consisted of a video for almost every DBT skill, with teaching from the Tees, Esk and

Wear Valleys NHS Foundation Trust DBT teams. It gave references to handouts available to buy online (which I could already access through my purchase of the DBT Training Manual). There was a very clear disclaimer that watching these videos did not constitute DBT treatment. They were designed as a learning resource to support those already undergoing DBT, or those who had completed a DBT programme.

It was only as I thought about the implications of this that I recalled having at one time been in a programme that included DBT. Back at New Beginnings in 2008 (thirteen years prior to this new exploration), I had been introduced to a variant of DBT intended for those with eating disorders. I remembered very little of it, as I had been so unwell during my time there, but I wondered if it qualified me to watch the DBT Skills Resource videos as one who had graduated a DBT programme.

Looking back it probably didn't, but I'm very glad that I decided to proceed, as the DBT Skills Resource and associated handouts proved to be a very effective means for me personally to learn DBT skills (without undergoing a full course in DBT). I have no doubt that in-person training with feedback from a skills trainer would be better for most people; however, at a time in my life when I was a new mum, and flexibility and accessibility were so important, the DBT Skills Resource proved to be the perfect solution.

During the spring of 2021, I completed the entire course – another marker of recovery. I watched one or two videos (each averaging twenty minutes) every evening, reflecting on what I was learning in a journal. A year on, I have just reread my entire journal, and it is clear to me that what I have been able to put into practice so far has helped me enormously, and there are skills I had forgotten that I want to revisit because I can see their relevance to ongoing situations in my life.

Skills that aligned with my faith

The purpose of DBT skills training is to empower students to gain mastery over their emotions, and, in so doing, to become more skilful and effective in interpersonal relationships. There are four skills modules: core mindfulness (comprising basic skills that underpin the skills in the other modules), distress tolerance (skills for surviving crises without making things worse), emotional regulation skills and interpersonal effectiveness skills. I worked through them in that order, jumping back and forward a little where related skills were cross-referenced between modules.

I understand why patients on most DBT courses spend longer on each skill and work through the modules at least twice. There is so much to discover, and the therapy is radically different from other talking therapies, notably, for me anyway, from the CBT I had tried before. I thought to myself that learning DBT skills felt much like being told to turn the other cheek (Matthew 5:39) must have felt to Jesus' disciples. The approach was so contrary to the principles I had tried to live by previously.

Despite my qualms about the basic worldview of the DBT design, I have discovered that the goals of the treatment – gaining mastery over emotions and becoming more skilful in relating to others – are in line with my Christian values. In fact, I can see how putting them into practice has helped me to become more Christlike, and in my own mind this was a parallel goal.

At the core of DBT is the aspiration to become more mindful; living in the present moment and participating fully in that moment rather than ruminating about the past or worrying about the future. DBT promotes that way of *being* I mentioned previously before advocating things you *do* to make life better.

I have written already about how I feel mindfulness is in line with the teachings of Jesus, who told us that 'each day has enough worries of its own' (Matthew 6:34). As I studied the DBT mindfulness skills, I realised I had not felt safe in the present moment. I thought I needed to plan for all eventualities in the future in case of unexpected trouble. I recorded in my journal that it is always safe to stay present because God holds the future, and I cannot control it: a life-changing lightbulb moment that has helped to free me from mental striving.

Engaging my 'wise mind'

The key mindfulness skill in DBT is called 'wise mind', and the goal of all DBT skills is to keep you tuned in to your wise mind as much as possible. The idea is that we all have a tendency to act from 'emotion mind', when feelings run high and drive us to act in a way that is less than self-controlled, or from 'reasonable mind', when we are cold and rational, and act in a way that helps us get what we want regardless of its effect on the emotions of others. Wise mind is where the emotion and reasonable minds overlap. We consider our emotions and our reasonable thoughts, and act in a way informed by both, using our intuitive wisdom and discernment.

As a Christian, I wanted to add to my wise mind a further element. I wanted to make sure that my actions were informed by Scripture and God's will for me, rather than just my own intuition. I think Marsha Linehan would have approved of this, as she wants her patients to harness all that is beneficial to them in terms of not acting purely out of 'hot' emotions or 'cold' reason. I have found that aspiring to being in a wise mind state has definitely helped me to be less impulsive and more careful about how I react in heated interactions or when making decisions.

Wisdom is, of course, valued above many other attributes in biblical teaching. 'Get wisdom,' says the writer of Proverbs again and again (4:5–7; 16:16; 19:8; 21:11). DBT has helped me make this goal central and has given me skills to help me realise it.

You read a little vignette at the beginning of this chapter in which I used skills to help me access my wise mind so I would not act in a way that might hurt others or make a crisis situation worse. At the beginning I was upset because of a small offence: Rob was late for the dinner I had prepared for us and, with underlying vulnerabilities – sleep deprivation, hunger, hormones – I was in emotion mind, at risk of acting impulsively and in a way that might have caused hurt on all sides.

Thankfully, DBT had helped me tune in to my inner weather patterns, to become aware of them, and that was empowering. I recognised I was in emotion mind and wanted to get into wise mind, but I could not just flick a switch. I needed skills.

Tolerating distress and regulating emotions

The first two skills I used were from the Distress Tolerance module, because I needed to buy myself time and survive the crisis moment – tolerating it without making the situation worse. 'STOP' is a first-line skill I have found useful again and again, even in apparently very minor crisis moments. It helps me to recognise what is going on and to take a breath before acting, so that when I do act, it is in a way that helps me to keep living in line with my goals and values, and prevents me from hurting others.

The second skill I used, the more dramatic 'dive manoeuvre', is something that, for me, has replaced emergency 'rescue medication' completely – to the extent that I no longer have even a backup prescription for the anxiety drugs I took for years. It is one of four DBT skills that change the body's biochemistry and engage the calming parasympathetic nervous system to quiet surging emotions, restoring a sense of peace and control. I find it quick and at least as effective as the fast-acting (but highly addictive) benzodiazepines I used to take when I felt overwhelmed and panicked.

The dive manoeuvre was developed by psychologists working with physiologists who understand the body's systems and how they react to extreme conditions. It involves holding the breath for thirty seconds while keeping your face in a sink or bowl of cold water. This tricks the brain into thinking you are diving and activates the parasympathetic nervous system to slow respiratory and heart rates, and quickly bring a sense of calm.

The next skill I used is simply called 'willingness' – a willingness to do 'just what is needed' in a particular situation. In Psalm 51:12, David prays: 'Restore to me the joy of your salvation and grant me a willing spirit, to sustain me.' Getting into wise mind is a biblical goal in itself. As Christians, we are also called to be willing to do what is needed and to know that this will sustain us.

Of course, the opposite of willingness is wilfulness, something associated with being stuck in emotion mind. When my emotions are hot, I do not want to tolerate distress; instead, I want to get my own way and do whatever feels good in the moment, such as getting one up on a person who has upset me with a sarcastic comment. In the process of learning DBT skills, I have observed my own wilful attitudes, and simply becoming aware of them has helped me channel my energies differently.

DBT teaches me to practise a wholehearted willingness to forfeit that sense of immediate reward in favour of preserving healthy relationships, again honouring my values and long-term goals. I can even adopt a posture that triggers my brain to act willingly, opening my hands and giving a half smile. These psychological tricks had never been taught to me in any other therapy, and I found that they do work, empowering me towards greater self-control – a fruit of the Spirit that has not always come naturally to me.

The skills I have described using so far all come under the category of distress tolerance. They get me through a crisis and back into wise mind, so I can use skills from the Emotional Regulation or Interpersonal Effectiveness modules to achieve my goals. What I really needed during the dinner table situation was to regulate my emotions to preserve a relationship that means a lot to me, through avoiding hurting Rob with a sharp comment.

DBT had taught me to 'check the facts' of the situation in order to guide my next steps. I identified that being upset about Rob's lateness was reasonable, but the surging emotions I was feeling were disproportionate, meaning that the right skill to choose was 'acting opposite' to them. It's very hard to maintain feelings of anger towards someone when you are doing something nice for them, so I made an empathetic comment and offered him a few extra minutes instead of doing what might have come more naturally and saying something snide.

As a result of studying DBT skills I have become gentler with others; more aware of the areas in my own life where I am at risk of sinfulness; and better able to judge the most important outcome in an interaction, be that getting my need met or maintaining self-respect. I am less insistent on being right, slower to judge others for what I interpret as their shortcomings and more understanding of the reasons why people behave the way they do. In short, the past year has seen me become humbler and more compassionate.

Skills and self-compassion

DBT has helped me to identify my values and to adjust my goals accordingly. It is because of DBT that I use fewer disposable baby wipes, recognising how much I value the environment.

DBT has changed my prayer life. It is because of DBT that I pray the Serenity Prayer ('God, grant me the serenity to accept the things I cannot change, the courage to change the things I can, and the wisdom to know the difference') in many situations on most days, rather than shooting so many 'Fix this!' arrow prayers upwards.

DBT has enabled me to become more resilient through 'investing in the bank of positive emotions'. It is because of DBT that I now plan family days out to beauty spots and open farms, and use spare moments to do something nice for a friend – even if it's just sending a picture of a bunch of flowers via WhatsApp.

I recognise that DBT is not for everyone. I also recognise that a Christian going into DBT treatment – especially full DBT rather than just the skills training I undertook – needs to be conscious that dialectics does not adequately describe the world in which we live.

When someone is emerging from mental illness, one of the first principles of recovery they discover is that recovery is very individual. It was only as I began to rediscover who Sharon was (as schizoaffective disorder – while still real – became a smaller part of my identity) that I recognised my tendency to feel strong emotions and sought a treatment that would help with this. Another person might identify a tendency to catastrophic thinking and find that, for them, conventional CBT is very useful.

What I would like readers to draw from this chapter is a realisation that we, as individuals who want to recover, can do a lot for ourselves that health professionals cannot offer. I found DBT skills and was empowered to take control of emotions I had been held captive by for years. There are opportunities out there, often without cost (other than time and commitment), to pursue all kinds of healthful activities that can enhance mental wellbeing.

I think of one friend who has found healing through gardening groups; another whose volunteering with the lonely has left her less isolated; another whose route to freedom from the trauma of living with psychosis has come through making art. My local recovery college helps people towards wellness through free courses on a range of topics from assertiveness training to journalling. Please be inspired to identify your own areas of need or weakness. Find out what is out there that might help, and don't reject things that may have potential just because they seem geared towards another group of people (with another diagnosis, for example, as in my case).

It was hard for me to acknowledge that I was unable to handle my irritations and frustrations in life healthily (or even my sadness, for that matter). I also found it difficult to talk about the extent to which hormonal cycling affected my moods. Today, I have compassion for myself in my struggles, but I also have the skills to overcome them – skills that had simply never been taught to me before. In other words, I can balance acceptance and change, and move forward in wisdom. That has been a major step towards greater wholeness; as a person and as a Christian.

Scripture and reflection

The wisdom that comes from God

At Gibeon the LORD appeared to Solomon during the night in a dream, and God said, 'Ask for whatever you want me to give you.'

Solomon answered, '. . . Now, LORD my God, you have made your servant king in place of my father David. But I am only a little child and do not know how to carry out my duties.

Your servant is here among the people you have chosen, a great people, too numerous to count or number. So give your servant a discerning heart to govern your people and to distinguish between right and wrong. For who is able to govern this great people of yours?'

The LORD was pleased that Solomon had asked for this. So God said to him, 'Since you have asked for this and not for long life or wealth for yourself, nor have asked for the death of your enemies but for discernment in administering justice, I will do what you have asked. I will give you a wise and discerning heart, so that there will never have been anyone like you, nor will there ever be. Moreover, I will give you what you have not asked for – both wealth and honour – so that in your lifetime you will have no equal among kings. And if you walk in obedience to me and keep my decrees and commands as David your father did, I will give you a long life.'

(1 Kings 3:5–14)

Solomon became king of Israel in around 970 BC, succeeding his father, David, who had been known as 'a man after [God's] own heart' (1 Samuel 13:14). He was anointed king at Gibeon, and in the verses above we read that God appeared to him in a dream there, offering him whatever he wanted.

Rather than health or wealth, Solomon asked for wisdom and discernment, and this pleased God greatly – so much so that he not only granted his request, but promised wealth and honour and, if he remained obedient, a long life as well.

Solomon did reign wisely for some years. He reorganised Israel's administration and rebuilt the Temple in Jerusalem, and extended Israel's influence through trade treaties. He wrote much of the book of Proverbs, sharing his wisdom with others based on the principle that 'the fear of the LORD is the beginning of knowledge, but fools despise wisdom and instruction' (1:7), and may also have contributed to other books of wisdom in the Bible, such as Ecclesiastes.

Solomon certainly accumulated the wealth and honour God had promised him, but ultimately proved unfaithful and disobedient, as his many wives brought with them foreign idols, which he also worshipped. This paved the way for the division of Israel and eventual failure of the monarchy.

Human wisdom is always faltering, but God's wisdom is perfect. As we read in James 3:17: 'But the wisdom that comes from heaven is first of all pure; then peace-loving, considerate, submissive, full of mercy and good fruit, impartial and sincere.' This is the kind of wisdom I crave. I want to be a woman of integrity; a woman who bears 'good fruit'.

As a Christian, I do not need to rely solely on the power of my own intuition. I ask God to help me to act from a place of wise mind, not driven by hot emotions or cool human reason, which may ignore others' feelings. The story of King Solomon shows that this kind of request pleases God, and that he will respond by granting wisdom and more. As I see it, DBT skills are tools that help me to drink from the wisdom of heaven. May I be pure and walk in obedience today!

Questions for personal reflection or discussion

1. Do you ever find yourself at the mercy of your emotions? Are you willing to commit to spending more time in 'wise mind' mode? Could you pray for wisdom today?

2. Are there any areas of your life where you feel you need new strategies or skills to be more competent and/or Christlike? What first step could you take towards wholeness?

7
Bearing fruit

Balancing acceptance and change

'In this world you will have trouble. But take heart! I have
overcome the world.'
(John 16:33)

Recovery principle 9
'Recovery is non-linear, characterized by continual growth
and improved functioning that may involve setbacks.'

Recovery principle 10
'Individuals . . . are empowered and provided the resources
to make informed decisions, initiate recovery, build on their
strengths, and gain or regain control over their lives.'

'At times our course is erratic, and we falter, slide back,
regroup, and start again . . . the aspiration is to live, work,
and love in a community in which one makes a significant
contribution.'[1]
(Pat Deegan PhD)

Spring 2022

*I zip my hoodie up a little higher as the wind blows my hair across
my face.*

*'Swing high, swing low, swinging everywhere we go. Swing high,
swing low, swinging everywhere.'*

I sing into the breeze, wondering whether my son can hear me at all.

He stretches out his palm as he swings towards me.

'Yay – high five!'

His smile is contagious. I laugh out loud.

'Hey, don't lean forward. You'll tip out! . . . Here, sit up – that's better.'

The swing wobbles sideways, caught in a gust. I wrinkle my nose as the smell of saltwater and seaweed wafts up from the beach. The sun comes out and the puddles glisten.

A little girl with long blonde hair runs towards us, followed by a mum pushing a baby in a pram.

'Hello! Are you coming to swing too?' I ask.

She nods, her chin touching her chest. Her mum smiles at me, parking her pram beside the climbing frame and lifting the girl into the baby swing next to my son.

'Look, here's a friend for you.'

He turns his head and grins.

'What do you call her?'

'Lucy – she's just turned three.'

'Wow, what a tall girl!'

Lucy's mum and I chat about the improvements to the park until we hear cries from the pram.

My phone beeps in my pocket and, between pushes, I pull it out to take a look. It's a reminder to pick up my medication.

'Okay, wee pet, we'll just swing ten more times and then Mummy needs to do her errands.'

Recovery is possible

Remember where I once was, not so very many years ago . . .

At times psychotic, haunted by an 'evil presence' and mocked by 'tormentors' no one else could hear or see . . . lonely in my deluded belief that professionals were trying to kill me and that the special messages I was getting were coming from a fourth dimension only I could access.

At times severely depressed, experiencing such profoundly low mood that my whole body slowed to a halt and even breathing seemed to hurt. Sometimes so distressed as to think life was not worth living; sometimes unable to think at all . . . and eventually treated with electroconvulsive therapy.

At times manic, lacking control over my own impulses and behaviours, acting uncharacteristically and causing embarrassment to myself and those around me. Thinking I was achieving great things, when actually I was leaving a trail of havoc I would need to redress after each episode.

I was stuck in a cycle of hospitalisations and discharges . . . experiments with different medications . . . hopes elevated and hopes dashed . . . drained and demoralised . . . dragging poor Rob with me on a lurching rollercoaster of emotions.

Perhaps you or a family member find this all too familiar. Perhaps mental illness dominates your life, and there seems to be no way out. Let me encourage you again by saying that things can change. They did for me, and I really believe there is potential for recovery in every individual, regardless of how hopeless the situation may appear.

Life looks very different for me today. It is purposeful. It is worthwhile. It is enjoyable.

I still live life aware that I have a severe mental illness. I still need to take medication – antipsychotics, two mood stabilisers, an antidepressant, even a drug to treat the inevitable side effects of the antipsychotics – and it leaves me tired and headachy at times.

I still have symptoms of depression, though I have been free of psychotic episodes for more than three years now.

Despite these realities, I feel no hesitation in saying that I am walking in recovery. Life is hard *and* life is good.

I am part of a family. I am a wife in a two-way relationship, in which my husband cares for my needs and I can care for his too. We love each other and share our hopes, dreams and decision-making. I am a mother at long last and can meet my son's needs in partnership with his daddy, enjoying all his little triumphs and comforting him when there are tears. I am also a daughter, a niece, an aunt, a cousin. I look to family members for support and encouragement, but I also contribute to their wellbeing, celebrating birthdays and achievements, and joining in prayer with those who struggle.

I am a member of a local church community. My church is a source of fellowship and offers opportunities for spiritual growth and discipleship. I can contribute in various small ways, whether by adding a package to the food bank trolley or praying for a suffering friend. I also receive in many ways, including through the preaching of the word, the prayers of faithful worshippers, and structured practical supports vital to raising our young child. I am growing in my faith, and one day hope to study the Bible in a more formal context, perhaps on a graduate theology course.

I am also a member of a local community of mums. I have met them in play parks, parent-and-toddler groups, soft-play sessions and even swimming pools. Some share my faith, many do not, but we all have a common bond as we journey through parenthood. Being a mum has given me links to the local library, relationships with Christians from other churches, insider knowledge about which cafés have the best highchairs and baby-changing facilities, and the reassurance that I am not alone in my worries about my little one.

I have hobbies and interests: I love to listen to contemporary Christian music; I enjoy getting stuck into the latest non-fiction book releases; I am passionate about the environment and relish making the most of the natural beauty around me. I may not have a lot of time for these things at the moment, but I can always enjoy small pleasures: a square of dark chocolate, an almond croissant, the smell of fresh coffee, my favourite grapefruit shower gel.

I have a meaningful career as a part-time writer and speaker. My main topics are faith, mental health and severe mental illness – areas I feel passionate about, and in which I want to encourage others. I engage with my readership and feel privileged that I have been given a platform from which to be a voice for the voiceless who live with psychotic illness. I enjoy the creative process and find reward in doing what I now believe God intended as a ministry for me.

I have other good friends too. I feel so blessed that friends from as far back as primary school remain part of my life, as do a few from my student days, several I've met through mental health services, and many from the churches I belonged to in Belfast before I moved to live with Rob. Some come to the seaside to hang out with my son and me, others make time for an evening chat on the phone. I value these friendships and prioritise investing in long-standing relationships even as I make new friends locally. Many of my oldest friends stood by me when I had little to give, and now I want to be there for them too in whatever way I can.

I do have mental illness, but I invest in all of these positive things as much as I can, so that the negative things – symptoms and side effects – have less power over me.

I am thankful for the extent to which my medications are working; I live by my WRAP; I practise yoga and mindfulness daily to manage my stress levels; and I use strategies and skills from DBT when my emotions become overwhelming.

Recovery is a continuing journey.

I am living the primary dialectic of recovery: balancing acceptance of ongoing symptoms and side effects with changing all that I can to modulate these same symptoms and side effects and make my life better.

Two things I am working on accepting . . .

Antipsychotics

Every single morning when our son wakes me or my alarm goes off, I find myself saying the same thing – sometimes quietly to myself, sometimes aloud to Rob – 'I hate antipsychotics!'

The old familiar grogginess makes it so hard to get out of bed, my head aches and I can barely think straight. I try to keep up a simple pitter-patter of chat with my son, but Rob knows that if he needs to ask me something he ought to wait fifteen minutes until I've had my coffee. Then he might get a sensible response.

By the time we sit down to breakfast, the coffee has worked and my head is usually a little clearer. I put my frustrations with the antipsychotics behind me and try to remember why I am so grateful for them. Without antipsychotics, it's almost certain I would not be well enough to enjoy family life.

Sometimes I feel the side effects throughout the day: the headache, excessive tiredness (though every mum I know is tired!), an antsy-ness in my legs. Sometimes I resent that I must take a further tablet three times a day to prevent more serious neurological problems that are associated with my drugs. Sometimes I worry about my risk of developing the chronic tics that can come with long-term use of the type of antipsychotic I take.

I am working hard on accepting that I am likely to need antipsychotic medication (and its antidote) for life; that I may never quite fire on all cylinders as I used to; and that I may eventually develop minor nervous system dysfunction at some point.

I'm still reasonably young, and it is quite a lot to take on board. I need to ask God for the serenity to accept what I cannot change again and again . . . and again. The fact is, antipsychotics have given me my life back, I cannot change their side effects, and recovery always involves compromise.

Blips

The other thing I am working on accepting is that recovery in this life is: first, non-linear; and second, never going to be perfect. I am going to have blips.

During the first two years of my recovery, I had brief battles with depression. I have written about the premenstrual exacerbation I experienced in chapter 6. For a week or two during many months, my mood dipped. However, it invariably returned to normal once my period arrived. In time I became quite resilient – I simply told myself things would be better by the end of the next week, and that, together with DBT skills, was enough to keep me going.

The third year has been different. Thankfully, I have still had no symptoms of psychosis or mania. However, I have had two significant and prolonged episodes of depression – worse before my periods but not lifting when they came. Neither was quite so serious as to make me believe that life was not worth living (as I had during episodes before my recovery), but both were debilitating.

The first, in the summer of 2021, lasted almost two months and really scared me. I thought I had put severe mood disturbance behind me, and its re-emergence made me desperately afraid that I would plummet into psychosis too – becoming unable to look after our baby.

I was less helpless than I had been in the past, however. I had a WRAP that allowed me to recognise the deterioration early, and I knew what I needed to do to get better again. I just hadn't tested it out before, so I lacked confidence that it would work. I also had DBT skills to help change my mood, but these were also untested.

I remember Olivia telling me one day: 'It's a cyclical condition. None of your episodes have ever lasted for ever. Just keep putting one foot in front of the other, and by the end of the day you'll be one day closer to feeling better again.' I felt less hopeful than she did, but I had little option other than to follow her advice, using my various tools and skills . . . until, one day, I did feel better again.

The second episode, at the beginning of 2022, was worse and went on for four months. I found myself fighting to hide tears from my son and bottling them all up during the day to cry in the evening once he was in bed. I still managed to enjoy him, but I enjoyed little else. I felt constantly exhausted and close to the end of my tether. Simple tasks seemed to require all the concentration and energy I could muster.

There was one evening when, in floods of tears, I told Rob I thought this episode – which had by then endured for almost three months – was going to end in hospitalisation. I seemed to be getting worse. Childcare was requiring all my reserves and I was starting to worry about becoming psychotic. He was calm and firm: 'We're not going to let that happen. I'm going to do more in the house, you're going to get more time to look after yourself. We're going to tackle this together.'

Just reaching that moment of near-crisis and acknowledging that things were bad seemed to trigger an instinct within me to use every recovery strategy I could muster. It may sound strange, but even though I felt so ill, I never for one moment thought I was no longer in recovery. I knew recovery was a journey, and that blips were an accepted part of that journey; this just happened to be the deepest valley yet.

Once I had gathered my composure, I had a moment of clear-headedness. This was my opportunity to try every skill I had developed, to put my WRAP into practice, to take advantage of all the helps and supports in the community around me. I told myself I was going to see this episode as a learning opportunity to establish what really worked best, so I wouldn't need to fall quite so far the next time depression hit.

Of course, I told my GP and psychiatrist I was struggling. It was important that I continued to communicate with my healthcare professionals, as recovery does not mean having to do everything on your own. I even agreed to a trial of an additional antidepressant, though eventually decided I had been managing better on my usual regimen.

All the while, I kept repeating three mantras: 'This too shall pass . . . Keep putting one foot in front of the other . . . You are one day closer to the end of this.'

Eventually, almost imperceptibly at first, things started to get better. I felt a little more energised day by day until I realised one mid-morning (often my worst time) that I actually felt good again, upbeat. That I was enjoying myself.

It has been really tempting for me to rail against these episodes of depression: 'This shouldn't happen to me – I'm in recovery!' I have realised, though, that with each episode that passes, I grow in confidence: 'I got through it before, and I can get through it again.'

I am learning to accept that I am having a bumpy year – that is my reality in this moment – and this is okay. I can still have a life worth living. Even throughout these bad times I have parented well, I have written well, I have contributed to the wellbeing of others. My investment in the positives has paid off, as the negatives associated with depression then have less power.

Contrasting traditional mental healthcare with a recovery-oriented approach[2]

Traditional mental healthcare: person re-experiences symptoms

Perceived deficit	Decompensation, exacerbation or relapse.
Intervention	Hospitalisation (perhaps involuntary), lecturing about poor compliance with treatment.

Recovery-oriented healthcare: person re-experiences symptoms

Perceived asset	Re-experiencing symptoms as a normal part of the recovery journey; an opportunity to develop, implement and/or apply coping skills, and to draw meaning from managing an adverse event.
Intervention	Expressing empathy and helping the person avoid a sense of demoralisation. Highlighting how long it may have been since symptoms previously reappeared. Providing feedback about the length of time it takes to sustain change. Offering advice on strategies to cope and reinforcing a sense of self-efficacy.

Two things I am working to change

Depression

Accepting in the present moment that I have an ongoing struggle with depression does not mean that I shouldn't take action to make things better. I have the serenity to accept that I feel a certain way; I have the courage to change my feelings and improve my mental health where I can.

This is my current journey. My trial of one additional antidepressant was not a success. I prepared myself for the possibility that I might need to consider another alternative; however, I have been reluctant to change the basic drug regimen that has been the foundation for my recovery. In light of that, I began to look into other options to address my prolonged low moods.

After doing some research online, I learnt that mindfulness-based cognitive therapy (MBCT) is now recommended by the UK's National Institute for Health and Care Excellence (which offers guidelines on the most effective treatments for every health condition) as a treatment for recurrent depression.

My diagnosis is no longer major depressive disorder, but depression is the most persistent symptom of my schizoaffective disorder. MBCT has been shown to be at least as effective as antidepressant treatment in preventing relapse in those with recurrent episodes of depression,[3] so I wanted to give it a try.

MBCT was not available in my local area, but I discovered that Professor Mark Williams, the clinical psychologist (and Anglican priest) who developed the treatment, had co-written a book with meditation teacher and journalist Dr Danny Penman, *Mindfulness: A practical guide to finding peace in a frantic world* (Piatkus Books, 2011). It presents MBCT as an eight-week course to follow independently, with accompanying audio tracks included with the purchase.

Being recovery-minded, I am always on the lookout for ways in which I can empower myself with tools to make my life feel even more worth living. I bought Professor Williams's book, and am currently halfway through the course.

I already feel that the techniques he presents are helping me detach from my depression, allowing it to come and go in waves without feeling overwhelmed or consumed by it. My mood has improved since I started the course, and even though I think I was already on an upward trajectory, I am hopeful that my new skills – such as 'body scanning' – will help me to stay well.

What is a body scan?

A body scan is a mindfulness meditation technique to calm the mind. It involves sitting or lying quietly, usually with eyes closed, and bringing conscious awareness to different parts of the body in sequence: toes, feet, ankles, lower legs, etc.

Rather than thinking *about* your feet, you *feel with* your feet, asking yourself which sensations you can directly sense there, such as contact with the ground, buzzing, tingling, warmth or cold. After scanning the whole body for sensations, you come to a point where you hold your entire body in conscious awareness, perhaps feeling tingling in the toes, pain in a shoulder, buzzing in the chest, cold in the fingertips . . . all at the same time.

It has a remarkably calming effect on the nervous system, and forms part of the treatment in both DBT and MBCT. I now frequently use a ten-minute guided version when I feel the need to soothe myself, and find that it works effectively, allowing me to move on with my day.

Anxiety

Something that has become clear to me in recovery is that I suffer from chronic anxiety. When I was cycling through episodes of schizoaffective disorder, the fact that I was anxious got missed again and again. It either seemed insignificant compared with the impact of psychosis or was thought of as secondary to the 'bigger' symptoms.

Now that I have had no psychotic experiences for more than three years and my mood has been less disturbed overall, the impact of anxiety has become evident. Learning how to recognise emotions through DBT was the first thing that alerted me to it. Take the example I used of Rob being late to dinner. At first I thought my heightened emotional state was due to irritation and frustration with Rob (and these were certainly contributing factors). However, as I compared the effects of the emotions with those listed in the DBT handouts for identifying emotions, I recognised that the strongest emotion I was feeling was, in fact, anxiety. I could not cope with being out of routine.

I had several lightbulb moments when I realised that my physical symptoms – palpitating heart, tingling legs, painful shoulders

– were due to anxiety; and more when I realised that my depressed mood was compounded by my anxiousness.

I discovered the work of an American psychiatrist, Judson A. Brewer MD, who had written a book about using mindfulness practices in the treatment of anxiety, and I wondered whether it would help me. *Unwinding Anxiety: New science shows how to break the cycles of worry and fear to heal your mind* (Avery, 2021) was a revelation to me. I learned to become curious about my anxiety when it hit me, as it is difficult to feel both curious and panicked at the same time, and found that 'breathing into' the places where I was holding my anxiety – mainly my shoulders and chest – helped to ease it.

As I scanned my body for signs of anxiety, I identified for the first time that my breathing was shallow for much of the day. I was hunching my shoulders up close to my ears and I was often clenching my jaw. All of these symptoms were transmitting feedback to my brain: 'I'm anxious!' and creating a feedback loop of worry and increased anxiety.

By becoming aware of this, I could consciously breathe more deeply, relax my shoulders and unclench my jaw, transmitting a 'no-threat signal' to my brain and breaking the feedback loop of worry, anxiety, more worry and more anxiety.

It sounds like a very simple trick, but it has helped me. I now recognise in my body when I'm feeling anxious; I breathe deeply into the areas where I am carrying the anxiety, holding those areas in a gentle, loving awareness (which sounds corny but actually works); and I deliberately change my breath pattern and posture.

There is much more to Dr Brewer's research, so I am really only at the beginning of my journey towards becoming less anxious, but I already feel less caught up in my anxiety. I can observe it and feel empowered to change my physiological responses to it.

The wisdom to know the difference

I accept that I need to take medications that have side effects I don't always like, and I accept that I am going to have blips at times.

However, I am choosing to change my vulnerability to low mood and my responses to anxiety.

But how do I know what I need to accept and what I need to change? Is it possible that I'm accepting or trying to change the wrong things? After all, at the time when I wrote *Wrestling with My Thoughts* in 2018, I made much of the fact that I accepted I was always going to live with severe mental illness. My challenge, as I saw it then, was to live well with my condition, and I did not expect that I would ever recover.

I think these are really difficult questions, and I believe it is important to maintain an ongoing practice of praying for wisdom; dialoguing with God about what it is right to accept, and where it is appropriate to try to change. I also acknowledge that God is sovereign, and it might not be his will for certain things to change. Perhaps I will always suffer depressive episodes, whether I practise MBCT or not. I don't yet know.

One thing I have learned in the past year, which I think is relevant to these questions, is the power of 'self-compassion'. This is a buzzword of recovery jargon that I really disliked when I first encountered it. I felt, as a Christian, that I experienced God's compassion and should demonstrate it to others; that only someone who had not experienced this heavenly compassion needed to show compassion towards him/herself.

I felt self-compassion was a concept informed by an inadequate worldview, and perhaps it is. However, Jesus taught self-love, another concept sometimes denigrated by Christians, but one that is assumed in the command to 'love your neighbour as yourself' (Matthew 22:39). Our Christian worldview informs us that God loves us and has compassion on us, but that doesn't mean we should not love or have compassion on ourselves.

I make mistakes. If I try to change something and it turns out I am pursuing the wrong path, I have two choices: be frustrated and disappointed in myself, or say to myself, 'It was understandable that you wanted to try that, and it must feel hard that it didn't work out – I'm sorry.' The first response leaves me in a place of suffering from which it is hard to recover; the second is self-loving, self-validating and self-compassionate. It allows me to grieve . . . and then move on.

Historically, I have been quite hard on myself as a person – quick to condemn and imposing high standards (and I believed this was appropriate for a Christian). The problem was, this left me dependent on supportive responses from other people when things were not going well for me, and this need was not always met. I floundered in a childlike state, not much use to others, until someone helped me get myself together again.

Today, I am able to approach myself differently. I realise that Christianity is a belief system completely dependent on grace, and that, if God is willing to show me grace, I need to be able to show grace towards myself. Now I can be self-compassionate, I have less need for others to show me compassion; I am less prone to being childlike and helpless; and I am much more capable of helping others.

I still pray for wisdom, and I find that, as discussed in chapter 6, God bestows it. However, if I do make a wrong decision I practise self-compassion, do something nurturing for myself and then ask for more wisdom to know how best to recover.

Recovery is an individual journey

I do not recount these stories of my efforts to accept some things and change others to provide a blueprint for everyone who seeks to recover. I don't see DBT, MBCT or Unwinding Anxiety as panaceas for all. One of the key principles of recovery is that it needs to be individualised.

You will have observed that I discovered early on that I liked mindfulness and it worked for me, and that this took me in a particular direction when looking for solutions to a range of problems. Mindfulness might not be for you. I know friends for whom CBT or psychoanalytical psychotherapy, for example, has kickstarted their recovery journey. They have found different books, courses and apps to help them, and these approaches are no less valid. The concept I want to share is that it is possible to take ownership of your recovery, to identify for yourself the areas in which you would like to see improvement, and to pursue solutions that work for you as a unique person.

I do think that, for those with severe mental illness at least, getting the right medications is critical. I see again and again that people get stuck because no combination they have tried has quite worked; because they are taking medication – perhaps of necessity – that disables them through sedation and emotional blunting; or because their health professionals do not see potential for their recovery, and enable them to accept too much disability.

If this is you or your loved one, please do not give up. I have no access to records that would allow me to list all the combinations of drugs I tried, but I am sure there were more than a hundred over the course of twelve years – more if you take into consideration the different dosing regimens. Eventually, my doctors got there. If I had not come to the point of realising I needed to compromise regarding side effects, they might never have got there.

It takes communication on all sides, teamwork, careful recording of successes and side effects, and most of all *hope* that it is possible for the person to get well again . . . but it can be done. The recovery journey can then begin in earnest.

At the same time, if your medication is not yet right, please don't think that you can't work towards recovery today. Every time you invest in a positive, every time you make a good life choice, every time you exercise self-care, you are journeying in recovery. Tell your healthcare team that you want recovery, ask them to adopt a recovery-oriented approach, and believe that recovery is possible for all.

My life was hellish and now it's a life worth living. It's not perfect, but I'm fulfilled and I have deep joy, and I'm hopeful that the future can be better still. There is no reason that, in time, you won't say the same.

What has helped my recovery?

The following is a summary list (in no particular order) of the factors that have contributed to my recovery to date:

- Hope: coming to believe that recovery was actually possible for me
- Medication: finally discovering an effective combination of drugs
- A therapeutic relationship: a full year of counselling
- A recovery mindset: determining to make every decision count towards recovery
- WRAP: developing and using a Wellness Recovery Action Plan
- DBT: learning and using skills to manage difficult emotions
- Mindful living: establishing a daily mindfulness practice and changing my 'way of being'
- Becoming more resilient: managing the blips more effectively
- Prayer: praying the Serenity Prayer daily, and having a small group of prayer supporters
- Church: being part of a community of believers and sharing my journey with them
- Key supporters: having a husband, family members and friends who have stuck by me
- Writing: sharing my journey to process my experiences and encourage others
- Balancing acceptance and change, and investing daily in the positives
- Major motivating factors, including needing to be well in order to parent well
- Improved gut health
- Encountering God in a new and profound way

Almost a year ago, my community mental health team, with my agreement, discharged me from their care. For many years I thought this team would be with me for life! It was a significant milestone on my journey, underlining that it was not just me who thought I was walking in recovery, but my health professionals recognised it too.

Dr Ken Yeow

What is resilience and how can the Church support people in developing it?

Resilience can be thought of as the ability to withstand and adapt to pressure. Another way of conceptualising it is in terms of the ability to return to a previous state of functioning after being subject to significant strain that has led to impairment of performance. In some cases, resilience is demonstrated through meaningful personal development in the midst of markedly challenging circumstances – something that has been described as 'post-traumatic growth'.

The Bible has quite a lot to say about resilience, particularly in relation to our walk of faith with God over time. Christians are called to fight the good fight. We are exhorted to have, by the grace of God, patience and perseverance in the midst of trials. He has promised to fulfil in us his good work of making us more like Christ, by the power of the Holy Spirit. The example of Jesus Christ himself – the One who sweat drops of blood while prevailing in prayer on the eve of the greatest rescue mission ever – stands out.

The Church can support people in developing resilience through its proclamation of the gospel of Christ itself. Through no merit of their own, humble believers can receive the life-changing affirmation and empowerment they need to live their everyday, often messy, lives. When a local Christian community can function with the level of love and unity it is called to and equipped for, the people within that group can experience a collective resilience that helps them cope better with whatever life throws up. If a specific church is able to impact its surrounding area with a positive and godly influence, whole segments of wider society could reap the benefits of a more patient, gracious and resilient culture.

Scripture and reflection

Recovery *works*

What good is it, my brothers and sisters, if someone claims
to have faith but has no deeds? Can such faith save them?
Suppose a brother or a sister is without clothes and daily food.
If one of you says to them, 'Go in peace; keep warm and well
fed,' but does nothing about their physical needs, what good
is it? In the same way, faith by itself, if it is not accompanied
by action, is dead.
(James 2:14–17)

When I was twenty-three years old, I went on a memorable young
adults' retreat where the title of the talks, focused on the New
Testament book of James, was 'Faith *works*'.

The key theme of the weekend was the idea, summarised above
in James 2:14–17, that we are saved by faith alone, but the outworking of true, transforming faith is good deeds. James writes in
verse 17: 'Faith by itself, if it is not accompanied by action, is dead.'

I think recovery is a bit like faith. If I had accepted that my new
medication had transformed my life back in 2018 and early 2019,
and then lived in the same way I had always done, my recovery
would have been dead. My life needed to show the outworking of
that inner transformation.

As when I came to faith, I had undergone deep change. The
chemical milieu of my brain had improved. But if I was going to
live a transformed life I needed to work at changing my mindset,
addressing past trauma, gaining new skills and reinvigorating my
relationships.

Today, I aim to work out my faith through the loving good deeds
that knowing Christ inspires me to do. I also aim to work out my
recovery through my commitment to finding and doing what
helps me to feel better. The more I feel better, the more capacity
I have to give to others, and the more I give to others, the more I
feel better.

In that sense, my faith journey and my recovery journey are deeply intertwined. As a Christian with severe mental illness, I feel it is impossible to have one without the other. My prayer for you, my readers, is that you can find faith, and with it the hope that is needed to start the process of building a life worth living.

Questions for personal reflection or discussion

1. Are you wrestling with uncertainty over whether you should accept or change something in your life? Is it possible that you might both accept it as it is now *and* work towards change? Could you pray for serenity, courage and wisdom today?
2. Is your faith journey evident to others through your works? If you are on a journey of recovery, how could you work towards building a life worth living today?

8

A new beginning

Recovery will be perfect

'Raised imperishable . . . in glory . . . in power . . . a
spiritual body.'
(1 Corinthians 15:42–44)

A new heaven and a new earth

Then I saw 'a new heaven and a new earth,' for the first heaven
and the first earth had passed away, and there was no longer
any sea. I saw the Holy City, the new Jerusalem, coming
down out of heaven from God, prepared as a bride beautifully
dressed for her husband. And I heard a loud voice from the
throne saying, 'Look! God's dwelling-place is now among the
people, and he will dwell with them. They will be his people,
and God himself will be with them and be their God. "He will
wipe every tear from their eyes. There will be no more death"
or mourning or crying or pain, for the old order of things has
passed away.'

He who was seated on the throne said, 'I am making everything new!' Then he said, 'Write this down, for these words
are trustworthy and true.'

He said to me: 'It is done. I am the Alpha and the Omega,
the Beginning and the End. To the thirsty I will give water
without cost from the spring of the water of life. Those who
are victorious will inherit all this, and I will be their God and
they will be my children.'
(Revelation 21:1–7)

An imperfect recovery

In previous chapters I have written of an imperfect recovery; a recovery that is not the same as 'cure'; a recovery that is a balance of acceptance and change. Today, I accept a certain level of depression and anxiety at times; I accept that medication saps some of my energy; I accept that there will probably always be certain things I need to do daily to stay well, sometimes at the expense of other things I might prefer to do.

As I have described, many different things have helped me attain this recovery. It began with a change initiated by health professionals, followed by the realisation that recovery was possible, and the motivation that came with becoming a parent. Several factors then increased my stability: developing a healthier relationship with God; living more mindfully; committing to a church and a community; accessing specific therapies; addressing physical illness; finding consistent prayer support; and investing in family connections and friendships.

It is wonderful to be in recovery, but I know that, in this life, my recovery will never be perfect. In this concluding chapter I want to write about my reawakening to the world around me, and about what I believe recovery will look like in the next life.

I look forward to a day when perfection will come, when I live in eternity with Christ.

We are told that our bodies will be 'raised imperishable . . . in glory . . . in power . . . a spiritual body' (1 Corinthians 15:42–44). Will I be 'cured'? That is something to which I have been giving a great deal of thought.

I have been on a journey of spiritual discovery over the past couple of years as I have become increasingly secure in my recovery, and recovery itself has caused me to re-evaluate the world around me.

Near-perfection in the world

During my first inpatient admission for depression, I wrote in my journal: 'The symphonies have lost their colour.' Depressed, music seemed bland to me, as did visual art, and indeed the natural world. For many years I walked about in a sea of neutrals . . . brown, beige, grey.

Now, in recovery, I am seeing the world in a new light; perhaps brighter than ever before in contrast with what I knew during those colourless times. And so much really seems near perfect.

I live in the Kingdom of Mourne where, as Percy French famously wrote, 'the Mountains of Mourne sweep down to the [Irish] sea'.[1] In the foothills there is a forest park, where I often walk with my husband and son on Sunday afternoons.

Last weekend, warm afternoon sunlight played on the carpet of red-brown leaves under the deciduous trees lining the riverbank path. I craned my neck to see the lofty tops of the evergreens beyond. The fronds of ferns at ground level echoed the spindly branches of the pines, while the gush of water blended with the constant hum of insects in the undergrowth. The air tasted fresh, the sky was clear. My heart welled up with joy and wonder at this apparently perfect scene.

In recovery, I see many things with renewed awe and wonder. What's more, I am also experiencing them through my son's excited eyes as he takes them in for the first time: Slieve Donard, Northern Ireland's highest peak, silhouetted black against pink skies; glass-like reservoirs brimming with icy drinking water; turbulent seas crashing over the town's promenade during storms. The natural world seems overwhelming in its majesty and raw power.

During a recent visit to an open farm, I felt as though I was encountering the animal kingdom in all its diversity for the first time. In my previously jaded mind, a sheep was a white woollen creature with little personality; here I met sheep of many colours and textures, with oval pupils in their big eyes, jostling to get seeds from our hands, some bullying the others to get more than their fair share. I saw cattle with gentle faces, rough-haired donkeys, cantering horses, squealing skewbald piglets, and I was struck by the differences and yet also the sameness I saw in all of these vital creatures.

As I read picture books to my son, I rediscover other landscapes: the Sahara Desert, tropical rainforests, even the crater-speckled moon! Beyond the moon, I encounter outer space, with its myriad stars and galaxies. Back on earth, I glimpse life beneath the seas, including brightly coloured creatures which, for years, no one could even see to appreciate. Blood rushes to my brain as emotion wells up within me. There is so much beauty, so much intricacy, yet for many years neither touched me, nor even registered with me at all.

I find it hard to see all of this and not believe it was designed. From the DNA that makes animals so different and yet so much the same, to snowflakes and diamonds, each unique, it seems to me that the evidence points to the existence of a Creator.

I'm writing now at Christmas, and my favourite feature of the season is the beautiful choral music it has inspired. Why do we have music? It's hard to think of it as something functional that gives us humans an evolutionary advantage. Instead, I find myself certain that it can only be a heavenly gift from a heavenly Creator.

There is so much in our world that is splendid and awesome, and now that I am in recovery, I appreciate it all as if for the first time. I feel overwhelmed by it at times, grateful, blessed.

And yet, something is clearly wrong.

An imperfect world

The most obvious evidence of this in my own experience is this sickness, this schizoaffective disorder, that has dogged me for so long. Now that I am in recovery, depression, mania and psychosis affect me so much less than they did, but I still have days when low mood and anxiety are pervasive and limiting, if no longer disabling.

Then there are the 'symptoms', if you like, that I used to attribute to my illness but now see as personal shortcomings: agitation, quickness to anger, tension, irritability, wilfulness, impatience, missed opportunities to do good. In the wider world, I see hatred and cruelty, war and abuse, oppression and fear.

Yet I also see good people, or at least people doing good. They show love and compassion, run food banks, volunteer with mental health charities, give of their money and their time. And I feel emotions that, by any standard, can be called good: joy, wonder, peace.

In recovery, I have asked myself where all this comes from, this good and this evil, these rights and wrongs. In the course of being unwell, I have at times become lost in the secular worldview and have seen why religion and ritual are often written off as outdated and anachronistic, even ridiculous. But every time I come back to the Bible I find the only explanation that makes sense . . .

A creator God who breathes perfection into pine trees and farm animals and sea creatures; who inspires music, paintings, drama and poetry. A cosmic war where evil forces, which began with the fallen angel we know as Satan, seek to spread darkness, malice and pain.

Even as I write, I think: *A fallen angel? Really? If God's creation was so perfect, how could that have happened?* It does sound like something out of a fantasy novel, and I don't have all the answers, but it's the only story that helps me to make sense of our world.

This world was always meant to be good, but evil distorted it. The beauty I see in creation was there from the beginning, from Eden, a perfect garden. That was all disrupted in the fall, when Satan, the master of lies, tempted Eve to eat the forbidden fruit. Since then, we have had sadness, suspicion, physical pain, cancer, death . . . and severe mental illness. I live in a world marred to this day by fallenness and despair, and I am reminded of it daily.

My body is imperfect. I need medication to control high blood pressure, my spine is inflexible because of old fractures, my diet is dictated by colonic dysmotility. The mental disturbances from which I suffered for so long have been well documented. For years I could find little peace, joy or hope (though I wrote about the glimmers that kept me going in *Wrestling with My Thoughts*).

Other people have different struggles: a terminal diagnosis, infertility, relationship breakdown, financial insecurity, children with additional needs. And that is only to list the experience of friends within my own circle. In the wider world, the last week's news reports have described desperate refugees, destructive tornadoes, war, homelessness, organised crime and child abuse.

A perfect Rescuer

When I was unwell, I found it hard to see beyond all this sorrow and pain in the world. It resonated so much with the sorrow and pain I felt inside. The 'noise' of all that was bad in the world drowned out the birdsong and the butterflies. But I read in the Bible that God never intended to allow the world to go on like this for ever. He had a rescue plan from the beginning.

Now experiencing this Christmas season anew as a mum to a little boy, I can begin to imagine Mary's emotions as she brought a baby into this imperfect world – a world in which her people, the Jews, were oppressed by Rome.

There is little doubt that this baby existed. Even secular historians believe that Jesus was born, lived a remarkable life and died on a cross. What if he really was the Son of God?

Sometimes I understand why the Jews rejected him. I find myself asking why he didn't come as a king. Did he really have to be so meek and lowly? But then I read again about the life of Jesus and see afresh his tenderness, gentleness and compassion; his radical teachings about loving our neighbour and giving our possessions to the poor; how he cared for little children, outcasts, lepers, the bereaved, the sick, the disabled, making the last first; how he delivered people from severe mental illnesses like mine; how he came indeed as a Wonderful Counsellor and Prince of Peace.

And I see those qualities today, imperfectly demonstrated in his people, ministering through churches, charities and individuals to the sick and the dying, to suffering children, to refugees, to the poor and the persecuted. During my own illness I have seen many personal expressions of care and support from ordinary Christians: hospital care packages; consistent, loving friendships; practical offers of lifts to and from hospital; home-cooked meals; people giving of their time to visit me; people faithful in prayer . . .

This little baby, this man, Jesus, the Christ, because of whom Christianity came about, made such an impact on the world. I see this and ask myself, *How could I ignore him?* I first committed my life to Jesus as a small child, struck by his love of little ones, his healings and his gentle face beaming at me from Bible picture books and flannel graphs. The words 'Suffer the little children to come unto me' (based on Matthew 19:14, Mark 10:14 and Luke 18:16) hung on a plaque above my bed . . . and I came to him.

In my teens I walked away for a time, more interested in the pleasures life outside the church had to offer. The witness of Christlike friends brought me back, and I got fired up by Jesus' message of salvation for all who would believe in his name and turn from their sin (John 1:12).

Then mental illness struck. Depression, tears, despair, mania, anorexia, loneliness and forgotten-ness almost consumed me. I became a psychiatric patient and lost my sense of identity as a child of God. I never stopped believing that he existed, but I felt he had abandoned me.

Mental illness became all that I could see. The arc of history with its promise of a kingdom – partially realised, but which will one day be completely fulfilled – was okay for others, but irrelevant to me.

Then I went to New Beginnings, and was overwhelmed by the care of Christians who showed me the Saviour's love, humility, gentleness, compassion and selflessness; and the generosity and loyalty of those back home, whose financial and emotional support was tangible and sustained. That was in 2008, and I have never turned my back on God again.

When I wrote *Wrestling with My Thoughts*, I was very much in the grip of mental illness, but there were tiny glimmers of hope. Now I find myself walking in true recovery, and hope dominates.

The Bible talks about the 'now' and the 'not yet' of the kingdom (Jesus teaches us to pray 'your kingdom come' in Matthew 6:10). Jesus has *now* been raised from the dead, making our salvation possible even as we live in an imperfect world, but he has *not yet* returned in power to rule the new, perfect, heaven and earth.

Recovery is possible in the now, but it is not the same as *cure*. It is not perfect. I believe that recovery in the 'not yet' will be truly perfect.

A perfect sacrifice

In the kingdom that has not yet come, we are promised that: "'He will wipe every tear from their eyes. There will be no more death" or mourning or crying or pain' (Revelation 21:4). That sounds a lot like an end to severe mental illness, doesn't it?

I used to think that, in heaven, in my perfect recovery, the stigmatising scars on my wrists would be gone . . . But Jesus had scars when he rose from the dead, which leads me to think that, while I might no longer cry, I might still carry the stigmata of mental illness in the fullness of God's kingdom.

The more I read the Bible, the more I see that the perfection of Eden will not be restored. Instead, the world will be transformed into something new and even more perfect, so to speak. This transformation began when Jesus died on the cross in place of his people and was raised to life in a miraculous process that brought victory over sin and evil, over Satan and his powers.

I grew up with this imagery, singing old songs with words such as 'there is power in the blood', which later made me cringe. The whole notion of blood sacrifice seems offensive to modern ears. I had to revisit the cross with the eyes of someone who had lived very much in a secular world; someone to whom the idea that one man's death could mean anything for all of humankind seemed odd and alien.

Rereading the whole Bible in a short time made it clearer to me: this was the pinnacle of the arc of history, God's story, Jesus' story – 'history is *his*-story', as I was taught in Sunday school. Like the Jews of Jesus' time, I had asked myself why Jesus hadn't come as a glorious king, but now it made sense. It's just the way God had set out for the powers of evil, which had come into the world at the fall, to be defeated. A gentle, perfect, 'ordinary' man (who was in fact the Son of God and not ordinary at all) had to take on the sin of all men and face death . . . only to overcome it and rise again to endless life.

The resurrection is a stumbling block for so many who look at the Christian faith and wonder if it's for them. How could that ever happen? Few deny the historical truth of Jesus' crucifixion, but many careful scholars who have examined the primary sources have also found convincing evidence for his resurrection.

However, for me, the evidence that Jesus didn't stay in the grave comes from what I see in the lives of those I know who follow him. Beginning with the first apostles, who faced all manner of persecutions and even death because of the message they brought – surely only because they truly believed in Jesus' resurrection – to all those Christians who have shown me such love and compassion, and indeed to my own heart, which I have seen changed into something much more tender and humble as I have trusted in Jesus.

The message of the apostles was that whoever believed in Jesus' death and resurrection, and that he was indeed the Son of God, would have eternal life beginning now, and that Jesus will come again, bringing a perfect kingdom where his followers will live in fellowship with him for ever, a new heaven and a new earth where there is no more sin.

Transformation, not restoration

What do I make of this promise of a perfect life beyond my death? I used to think it followed that I would have no trace of mental illness – that I would be restored to how I was before I developed any symptoms, and my scars would disappear.

But then we have the fact that Jesus' scars remained when he appeared to his disciples after his resurrection, despite the fact that he clearly had a new body, which was not constrained by physical barriers. We know this because he could pass through the wall of the upper room.

Would it really be heaven for me if I still had scars? Is it possible that I might bear other remnants or reminders of mental illness?

I will certainly be identifiable, but is there enough 'Sharon-ness' without them? It seems less important to me now . . .

We read in 2 Corinthians 3:18: 'And we all, who with unveiled faces contemplate [Jesus'] glory, are being transformed into his image with ever-increasing glory, which comes from the Lord, who is the Spirit.'

Recently, I have begun to realise that God is not restoring me; he is transforming me. My journey through illness has been painful, agonising at times, but it has moulded me into a different, kinder, more empathetic, gentler person than I was before I became unwell. On reflection, I don't want to lose any of those more Christlike characteristics.

Severe mental illness has been unwelcome, but there is no doubt that God has been redeeming my struggles in many ways – including through my writing, which has allowed me to connect with and minister to others who have had similar experiences.

I believe that heaven will be perfect. All those scenes of apparent near-perfection I see around me now – the snowflakes and the pine trees, the animals and the galaxies – will be surpassed by the absolutely perfect scenes in the new heaven and new earth.

The apostle John, who described a vision of heaven he was given in the final book of the Bible, Revelation, could not find words to match what he saw. He wrote of gold, jasper, sapphire, emerald; of creatures with wings, covered in eyes; of dazzling light and pearly gates . . . but he only had human language at his disposal. Surely he did not do justice to the amazing beauty of what he actually saw.

I find myself asking, in light of all this perfection, whether my scars will really matter in heaven. They will tell a story, but ultimately it will be a story of truth, fulfilment and redemption. No one will judge me, because Jesus has declared me perfect. I may carry the stigmata of mental illness, as Jesus carries the stigmata of crucifixion, but I will not weep and I will not mourn.

Shalom: perfect peace

In Hebrew there is a word for perfect peace, 'shalom', which is often used as a greeting. It signifies wholeness, completeness, true wellbeing.

I believe I will have eternal, all-encompassing shalom when I get to heaven. I will be so awed, so comforted and so complete in the presence of God, my Creator, that mental illness will have no power. It will not matter.

All the things that have gone along with it in a cycle of exacerbation and remittance – wilfulness, agitation, irritability, anger and emotional lability – all signs of my sinful nature, will be completely eradicated, as I will have been transformed into the likeness of Christ. They will be replaced with willingness, calm, patience, peace, stability and serenity. There will be no depression to cause me to cry, nor mania to cause me to act inappropriately, nor psychosis to disrupt my peace.

This week, a beautiful Christian friend of mine lost her battle with mental illness. She did not know recovery here on earth. I am comforted to know that, today, in the perfect heaven where she is held in the arms of her perfect Saviour, she knows perfect shalom. She will never know torment again. She has total comfort, total security and absolute peace.

Perfect recovery is for all Christians

For a long time, mental illness was my identity. In certain circumstances, I even introduced myself this way: 'I'm Sharon, and I have schizoaffective disorder'! In recovery here on earth, I have developed a healthy identity as a child of God with many attributes, including that I have a diagnosis of severe mental illness. In heaven, I will simply belong to Jesus, and mental illness will no longer have any power.

The perfect recovery I will know in heaven is for all Christians with mental illness – for those who, like me, find an imperfect recovery on earth, and for those who, like my dear, dear friend, do not see recovery in this lifetime.

There are many things we can learn from the recovery model of mental healthcare: that it is possible for life to be better; that by investing in the positive aspects of life we can reduce the impact of the negative aspects; that our journeys are individual and our path towards healing must be adjusted according to our own strengths and weaknesses . . . to name but a few.

But let me leave you with this recovery model message: there is always hope, even in this imperfect world. And for Christians, who look forward to one day being made perfect, this message is amplified ten thousand times.

Please, please, never give up hope. Instil it in your friends, share it with your colleagues, hang on to whatever glimmers you have yourself. For me it took time, but recovery came, and I know that shalom will follow.

Scripture and reflection

Eden restored

Then the angel showed me the river of the water of life, as clear as crystal, flowing from the throne of God and of the Lamb down the middle of the great street of the city. On each side of the river stood the tree of life, bearing twelve crops of fruit, yielding its fruit every month. And the leaves of the tree are for the healing of the nations. No longer will there be any curse. The throne of God and of the Lamb will be in the city, and his servants will serve him. They will see his face, and his name will be on their foreheads. There will be no more night. They will not need the light of a lamp or the light of the sun, for the Lord God will give them light. And they will reign for ever and ever.

(Revelation 22:1–5)

I quoted Psalm 88 in the Introduction. The author ended his prayer with the words: 'Darkness is my closest friend.' He knew deep depression, and God was able to handle that. He did not need the prayer to end with a hopeful expression of trust as other lament psalms do. I wonder what the writer of Psalm 88 would have made of Revelation 22:5. Here, we have a promise of endless, radiant light – an end to darkness, an end to night. The psalmist could not see beyond his current circumstances, but the God to whom he prayed knew that darkness would not triumph in the end.

He, the Lord of light, will return on a day when some of his people are mired in darkness; when they feel as though they have no closer friend. On that day, their lament will turn to rejoicing as the forces of darkness and depression are overcome by marvellous light: 'No longer will there be any curse' (Revelation 22:3).

Sometimes, during the darkest days of my illness, I felt as though the darkness was keeping me from God's love. In Romans 8:35–39, the apostle Paul insists this could never be the case:

> Who shall separate us from the love of Christ? Shall trouble or hardship or persecution or famine or nakedness or danger or sword? . . . No, in all these things we are more than conquerors through him who loved us. For I am convinced that neither death nor life, neither angels nor demons, neither the present nor the future, nor any powers, neither height nor depth, nor anything else in all creation, will be able to separate us from the love of God that is in Christ Jesus our Lord.

I could paraphrase verse 35 as follows: 'Who shall separate us from the love of Christ? Shall depression or mania or psychosis or anxiety or eating disorders or suicide?' and still the answer would be: 'No. *Nothing* will be able to separate us from the love of God that is in Christ Jesus our Lord.'

The central aim of the mental health recovery model is to help people to build 'a life worth living'. Christians are promised this and so much more – that they will drink 'from the spring of the water of life', which is 'as clear as crystal' (Revelation 21:6; 22:1), and reign with God in the kingdom of light for eternity (22:5).

Now that, in my view, is a picture of true recovery.

Questions for personal reflection or discussion

1. What is the greatest evidence in your life that we live in an imperfect world? What does it (or would it) mean to you to know that Jesus' death and resurrection has redeemed your suffering?
2. What makes your life worth living? What is the next step you need to take in your recovery journey?

Epilogue

It is almost a year since I submitted my first full draft of *Tending to My Thoughts*, and a lot has happened since then! My recovery journey has had its ups and downs, but I have kept my focus, and the general trajectory is towards wholeness.

However, I think it is important to mention that the months following my submission were difficult. Outwardly, I appeared calm and in control, parenting and writing as usual. Inwardly, I was struggling with a deeper depression than I had experienced in several years.

I questioned myself: *How can I publish a book on recovery when I feel so unwell?*

It came down to having confidence in the truths I had explained in the book. Recovery is not a linear path; it's a mindset. Recovery is not about being 'cured'; it's a daily commitment to doing the next small thing that helps. Symptoms continue. Treatments are necessary. But life has purpose and meaning.

You've read a lot about the things I discovered I could do for myself to promote recovery. All of these were – and *are* – useful and important . . . but in the past year I have had to acknowledge that recovery needs to be a collaborative process. Therapeutic relationships are vital.

My depression became more than I could handle alone. I was not completely dysfunctional, I was not suicidal. But every day was just about 'getting through'. I felt awful, and I could not enjoy my family, my work or God. I came to accept that my medication needed to be reviewed.

The outcome was that, in partnership with my doctors, I embarked on lithium therapy – something intended to be lifelong, and it wouldn't be a quick fix. For the first couple of months I felt tired, headachy and groggy. Then the dose was reduced and I began to feel better. I was no longer simply surviving my days; instead, I began to look to the future with hope.

I wanted to share this because readers need to know that you don't always have to *feel* recovered to be walking in recovery. And although I have encouraged you to take responsibility for making recovery-orientated choices, such choices must include seeking appropriate help when necessary.

I was not a failure because my mental health deteriorated; in fact, I chose to see the deterioration as an opportunity to learn new things about myself and about what I needed to do to stay well.

I learned a lot! I learned that I could not take on writing commitments at the expense of self-care activities. I learned that I needed to revisit my WRAP plan regularly – and stick to it. I learned that I wasn't always the best person to decide what I needed at times of vulnerability.

Emerging from this prolonged depressive episode in December 2022, I determined to do all that I could to bolster my mood in 2023. I changed my gym membership to make it more flexible and started taking regular aerobic exercise again. The endorphins helped, and so did getting out of the house in the evenings. I wanted to focus on parenting and family, so I reduced my writing commitments.

* * *

It's a few months on now, so where am I today? Still a little fragile, but much more assured in my recovery. I am still using many of the techniques I've described in these pages – practising self-compassion, breathing into anxiety with a curious mind, body scanning, mindful yoga, paced breathing and progressive muscular relaxation . . . and more (not all of them every day, of course, but drawing from my toolkit!). I am also intentionally seeking to grow in faith as I walk this recovery road. For example, I have rediscovered Christian radio, and I've just been gifted access to some exciting online Bible study resources.

Epilogue

I went back to the recovery college this term, taking three short courses I felt might help me to manage my darker days more effectively. The most relevant of these was 'Living Life to the Full', a series of six seminars designed to equip those with chronic depression to live meaningful lives.

The skills it teaches are simple – for example how to break the vicious cycle of doing less, feeling worse and doing still less – through making small changes like reintroducing something you used to find pleasurable into your daily routine. I found these skills useful. It was also good to meet (via Zoom) with others who had similar struggles but were committed to recovery.

These courses are important, but there are a lot of other things going on in life today that contribute to my wellness and, at times, add to my stress! I must choose daily to make time for mindfulness practices that help me stay aware of the direction of my thoughts, the ebb and flow of my emotions, the alignment – or otherwise – of my decisions with my values, and my general state of wellbeing – and what I might need to do to reorientate myself towards recovery.

I find mindfulness practice, and its overflow into mindful living, to be of prime importance. For me, being mindful of God's work and voice in my life, and ensuring I am in step with his plans, is a natural overflow of this 'secular' practice (as Dr Yeow highlighted in his expert view).

Today, I find myself looking to the future. I am enjoying life as a wife and mum, and as a part-time writer, but new things lie ahead. Our son will soon start preschool, so I'm going to have more time on my hands. Will I write another book? Will I look for a part-time job? Will I embark on deeper theological study?

Mindfully, I'm seeking God's will, thinking about my values and remaining aware of my thoughts, emotions and behaviour. I find it difficult to live day to day without a clear map of the way ahead, but I'm acknowledging that and committing to stay present in the here and now, while also tuning in to the advice of others, and to my innermost desires, about the future.

One thing that is very dear to my heart, and will be a priority in the years to come, is launching and promoting this book . . .

because I want to give everyone with mental illness hope of the recovery I have come to know. In the here and now of today, I am mindful that I value the wellbeing of others and am deeply committed to imparting hope. I believe that this is consistent with God's plan for me going forward.

So, whenever you are reading this, be sure that my prayer for you is that you will grasp the truth that recovery is possible – through small decisions, small changes in mindset and small steps – even where hope is faint and the struggle is great. Be open to it. Approach it in your own way. Stick with it even when you feel as though you're floundering. Reach out to others who believe in recovery. Reach upwards to the God of all hope who offers freedom in the now and in the not yet.

Thank you for having the openmindedness to finish this book. My story isn't over; neither is yours. So let's do this together! One mindful choice at a time.

Appendix
Useful resources

For comprehensive information on mental illness, including schizophrenia, bipolar disorder and schizoaffective disorder:

The Royal College of Psychiatrists (UK)

www.rcpsych.ac.uk/mental-health

'Readable, user-friendly and evidence-based information on mental health problems, treatments and other topics, written by psychiatrists with help from patients and carers.'

Mind

www.mind.org.uk

'We won't give up until everyone experiencing a mental health problem gets support and respect.'

Rethink

www.rethink.org

'We improve the lives of people severely affected by mental illness through our network of local groups and services, expert information and successful campaigning.'

For mental health advice from a Christian perspective:

The Mind and Soul Foundation
www.mindandsoulfoundation.org

'To equip, educate and encourage.'

For churches seeking to offer support to those with mental illness:

Alan Thomas, *Tackling Mental Illness Together: A biblical and practical approach* (London: IVP, 2017). A helpful book written by a psychiatrist for Christians who are not mental health professionals but want to make a difference for people with mental illness. Accessible and empowering.

Christopher C. H. Cook and Isabelle Hamley, eds, *The Bible and Mental Health: Towards a biblical theology of mental health* (London: SCM Press, 2020). An academic but very readable resource.

Kintsugi Hope

www.kintsugihope.com

'A world where mental and emotional health is understood and accepted, with safe and supportive communities for everyone to grow and flourish.' Kintsugi is a Japanese technique for repairing pottery with seams of gold. Kintsugi Hope Wellbeing Groups 'enable churches to reach their congregations and communities to support people's mental and emotional wellbeing.'

The Sanctuary Course

www.sanctuarymentalhealth.org/sanctuary-course

'The Sanctuary Course is a study guide for small groups, designed to raise awareness and start conversations in local churches regarding mental health.'

Mental Health First Aid

https://mhfaengland.org

Training in appropriate first responses for different mental health-related situations.

For anyone interested in learning more about mental health recovery:

Check out the website of your local health trust for details of free courses open to all through their recovery college. You can also take free online courses from anywhere in the UK through the website: www.recoverycollegeonline.co.uk.

The American Psychiatric Association offers free online training videos on recovery-oriented mental healthcare here: www.psychiatry.org/psychiatrists/practice/professional-interests/recovery-oriented-care.

Other helpful Christian books on mental health

Mark Meynell, *When Darkness Seems My Closest Friend: Reflections on life and ministry with depression* (London: IVP, 2017). A pastor, speaker and writer seeks to find words for those whose depressive illness has left them speechless. This is a deeply personal story as well as a compendium of resources for 'fellow cave-dwellers', particularly focused on Christian leaders, but with wisdom for all.

Emma Scrivener, *A New Name: Grace and healing for anorexia* (London: IVP, 2012) and *A New Day: Moving on from hunger, anxiety, control, shame, anger and despair* (London: IVP, 2017). Beautifully written accounts of finding Jesus amid an agonising personal struggle with mental illness. Emma inspired me to write my own story.

Kathryn Greene-McCreight, *Darkness Is My Only Companion: A Christian response to mental illness* (Grand Rapids: Brazos Press, 2015). Greene-McCreight, a respected theologian with bipolar disorder, writes: 'This project examines the distress caused and the Christian theological questions raised by a clinical mental illness, namely, mine.'

Paul Ritchie, *Is It Unspiritual to Be Depressed? Loved by God in the midst of pain* (Fearne: Christian Focus Publications, 2022). A pastor who lives with OCD and depression shares his story and reflects on some of the questions Christians with mental illness often have. Honest, gentle and easy to read.

Rachael Newham, *Learning to Breathe: My journey with mental illness* (London: SPCK, 2018) and *And Yet: Finding joy in lament*

(London: Form, 2021). A young theologian and mental health advocate who struggles with depression, self-harm and disordered eating finds hope and joy in God. It's worth being aware that *Learning to Breathe* is sometimes graphic.

Two enlightening accounts of severe mental illness from a secular perspective:

Elyn R. Saks, *The Centre Cannot Hold: My journey through madness* (New York: Hachette Books, 2007). A law professor's story of living with schizophrenia.

Kay Redfield-Jamison, *An Unquiet Mind: A memoir of moods and madness* (London: Picador, 1995). A professor of psychiatry shares her journey with bipolar disorder.

If you or someone you know needs immediate emotional support, the following helplines are available (in the UK):

Premier Lifeline: The national Christian helpline: 'Being there at the end of the phone line. A place where faith and compassion meet.' Call 0300 111 0101 between 9 am and midnight every day.

The Samaritans: 24-hour telephone (116 123) and email (jo@samaritans.org) helplines.

Saneline: 'We believe no one affected by mental illness should be alone when they face crisis, distress or despair.' Call 0300 304 7000 between 4 pm and 10 pm every day.

In an emergency

If you or someone else has thoughts of suicide, or of harming themselves or others, it is a mental health emergency, and you should call 999 or attend the nearest emergency department. In less urgent situations, phone your GP or contact the local out-of-hours service. In England and Wales, call 111.

Notes

Epigraph

1 C. S. Lewis, from *Letters of C. S. Lewis* (London: Fount Paperbacks, 1988).

Prologue

1 'Recovery-Oriented Care in Psychiatry: Module One: Introduction', American Psychiatric Association: https://www.psychiatry.org/psychiatrists/practice/professional-interests/recovery-oriented-care (accessed 10 August 2023).

Introduction

1 Recovery principles at the start of each chapter are based on those outlined by the Substance Abuse and Mental Health Services Administration (SAMHSA) in 'SAMHSA's Working Definition of Recovery: 10 guiding principles of recovery', August 2010: https://store.samhsa.gov/sites/default/files/d7/priv/pep12-recdef.pdf (accessed 10 August 2023).

2 'Schizophrenia', Rethink Mental Illness: www.rethink.org/advice-and-information/about-mental-illness/learn-more-about-conditions/schizophrenia (accessed 10 August 2023).

3 'Psychosis', Mind: www.mind.org.uk/information-support/types-of-mental-health-problems/psychosis/about-psychosis (accessed 10 August 2023).

4 'Bipolar – the facts', Bipolar UK: www.bipolaruk.org/FAQs/bipolar-the-facts (accessed 10 August 2023).

5 'Schizoaffective Disorder', Rethink Mental Illness: www.rethink.org/advice-and-information/about-mental-illness/learn-more-about-conditions/schizoaffective-disorder (accessed 10 August 2023).

6 Centre for Evidence-Based Medicine. 'Severe mental illness and risks

from COVID-19', CEBM, 5 August 2020: www.cebm.net/covid-19/severe-mental-illness-and-risks-from-covid-19 (accessed 10 August 2023).

7 K. Hall, 'Understanding Validation: A way to communicate acceptance', *Psychology Today*, 26 April 2012: www.psychologytoday.com/gb/blog/pieces-mind/201204/understanding-validation-way-communicate-acceptance (accessed 10 August 2023).

1

1 R. Diamond, quoted in the Introduction of 'Recovery-Oriented Care in Psychiatry – Module One', American Psychiatric Association: https://www.psychiatry.org/psychiatrists/practice/professional-interests/recovery-oriented-care (accessed 10 August 2023).

2 American Psychological Association and M. A. Jansen, 'Recovery to Practice Initiative Curriculum: Reframing Psychology for the Emerging Health Care Environment', American Psychological Association, August 2014: https://www.apa.org/pi/mfp/psychology/recovery-to-practice/all-curriculums.pdf (accessed 10 August 2023).

3 American Psychological Association and M. A. Jansen, 'Recovery to Practice Initiative Curriculum'; Leamy et al., 'Conceptual Framework for Personal Recovery in Mental Health: systematic review and narrative synthesis', *The British Journal of Psychiatry*, vol. 199 (December 2011), pp. 445–452.

4 SAMHSA, *SAMHSA News, vol 4*, January–February 2006, p. 25.

5 'SAMHSA's Working Definition of Recovery'.

6 W. A. Anthony, 'Recovery from Mental Illness: The guiding vision of the mental health system in the 1990s', *Psychosocial Rehabilitation Journal*, 16(4), pp. 11–23.

7 'SAMHSA's Working Definition of Recovery'.

8 American Psychological Association and Jansen, 'Recovery to Practice Initiative Curriculum'.

9 Leamy et al., 'Conceptual Framework for Personal Recovery in Mental Health'.

10 J. Piper, 'What Is So Important About Christian Hope?' Desiring God, 7 March 2008: https://www.desiringgod.org/interviews/what-is-so-important-about-christian-hope (accessed 10 August 2023).

11 P. Deegan, quoted in 'Recovery-Oriented Care in Psychiatry: Module One'.

2

1 M. Ragins, quoted in 'Recovery-Oriented Care in Psychiatry – Module One'.
2 'Psychosis', NHS UK: www.nhs.uk/mental-health/conditions/psychosis/overview (accessed 10 August 2023).
3 'Antipsychotics: what is the science behind antipsychotics?', Mind: www.mind.org.uk/information-support/drugs-and-treatments/antipsychotics/about-antipsychotics (accessed 10 August 2023).
4 'Antipsychotics', Mind.
5 T. Stargardt et al., 'Effectiveness and Cost of Atypical Versus Typical Antipsychotic Treatment for Schizophrenia in Routine Care', *The Journal of Mental Health Policy and Economics*, vol. 11 (June 2008), pp. 89–97.
6 'Prescribed Medicines Review Summary', Public Health England: www.gov.uk/government/publications/prescribed-medicines-review-report/prescribed-medicines-review-summary (accessed 10 August 2023).
7 E. Penn and D. K. Tracy, 'The Drugs Don't Work?: Antidepressants and the current and future pharmacological management of depression', *Therapeutic Advances in Psychopharmacology*, vol. 2 (October 2012), pp. 179–188.
8 Fournier et al., 'Antidepressant Drug Effects and Depression Severity: a patient-level meta-analysis', *JAMA*, vol. 303 (6 January 2010), pp. 47–53.
9 'Antidepressants', Mind: www.mind.org.uk/information-support/drugs-and-treatments/antidepressants/about-antidepressants (accessed 10 August 2023).
10 'Your Guide to Medication: Agomelatine', Young Minds: www.youngminds.org.uk/young-person/medications/agomelatine (accessed 10 August 2023).
11 'Antidepressants', Mind.
12 'Lithium and other mood stabilisers', Mind: www.mind.org.uk/information-support/drugs-and-treatments/

lithium-and-other-mood-stabilisers/about-mood-stabilisers (accessed 10 August 2023).

13 K. Soares-Weiser, et al., 'A Systematic Review and Economic Model of the Clinical Effectiveness and Cost-Effectiveness of Interventions for Preventing Relapse in People with Bipolar Disorder', *Health Technology Assessment*, vol. 11 (October 2007), pp. iii–iv, ix–206.

14 C. Swindoll, 'First Peter', Insight for Living Ministries: https://insight. org/resources/bible/the-general-epistles/first-peter (accessed 10 August 2023).

15 J. Piper, 'Long for the Pure Milk of the Word', Desiring God, 30 January 1994: www.desiringgod.org/messages/long-for-the-pure-milk-of-the-word (accessed 10 August 2023).

3

1 American Psychological Association and Jansen, 'Recovery to Practice Initiative Curriculum: Reframing Psychology for the Emerging Health Care Environment'.

2 'Postnatal Depression and Perinatal Mental Health', Mind: www. mind.org.uk/information-support/types-of-mental-health-problems/ postnatal-depression-and-perinatal-mental-health (accessed 10 August 2023).

3 L. M. Howard and H. Khalifeh, 'Perinatal Mental Health: A review of progress and challenges', *World Psychiatry*, vol. 19 (October 2020), pp. 313–327.

4 'Postpartum Psychosis', NHS UK: www.nhs.uk/mental-health/ conditions/post-partum-psychosis (accessed 10 August 2023).

5 L. M. Howard and H. Khalifeh, 'Perinatal Mental Health'.

6 'Postpartum Psychosis', NHS UK.

7 'Treatment – Postnatal Depression', NHS UK: www.nhs.uk/mental-health/conditions/post-natal-depression/treatment (accessed 10 August 2023).

8 'Postpartum Psychosis', NHS UK.

9 'Postnatal Depression and Perinatal Mental Health', Mind.

10 Wesseloo et al., 'Risk of Postpartum Relapse in Bipolar Disorder and Postpartum Psychosis: A systematic review and meta-analysis', *The American Journal of Psychiatry*, vol. 173 (February 2016), pp. 117–27.

11 'Postnatal Depression and Perinatal Mental Health', Mind.

12 L. M. Howard and H. Khalifeh, 'Perinatal Mental Health'.

4

1 G. McConville in C. C. H. Cook and I. Hamley, *The Bible and Mental Health: Wholeness and illness* (Conclusion), (London: SCM Press, 2020), p. 31.

2 'Holy', Merriam-Webster: https://www.merriam-webster.com/dictionary/holy (accessed 10 August 2023).

3 'Qodesh', Bible Study Tools: https://www.biblestudytools.com/lexicons/hebrew/kjv/qodesh.html (accessed 10 August 2023).

4 NIV Study Bible (Grand Rapids, MI: Zondervan, 1985), p. 933.

5

1 P. Deegan, quoted in 'Recovery-Oriented Care in Psychiatry – Module One'.

2 For more information about WRAP, visit www.wellnessrecoveryactionplan.com.

3 'Jon Kabat-Zinn: Defining Mindfulness', Mindful, 11 January 2017: www.mindful.org/jon-kabat-zinn-defining-mindfulness (accessed 10 August 2023).

4 The information in this section is taken from T. Ireland, 'What Does Mindfulness Meditation Do to Your Brain?' *Scientific American*, 12 June 2014: https://blogs.scientificamerican.com/guest-blog/what-does-mindfulness-meditation-do-to-your-brain (accessed 10 August 2023).

5 'Yoga', Collins English Dictionary: www.collinsdictionary.com/dictionary/english/yoga (accessed 10 August 2023).

6

1 M. M. Linehan, *Building a Life Worth Living: A memoir* (New York, NY: Random House, 2020), p. 29.

2 'Dialectic' Oxford Languages and Google: https://www.google.com/search?q=dialectic (accessed 10 August 2023).

3 M. M. Linehan, *Cognitive-Behavioural Treatment of Borderline Personality Disorder* (New York, NY: Guilford Press, 1993), p. 31.

4 M. M. Linehan, *DBT Skills Training Manual* 2nd edn (New York, NY: Guilford Press, 2015), pp. 286–89.

5 Linehan, *DBT Skills Training Manual*, p. 5.

7

1 P. Deegan, quoted in 'Recovery-Oriented Care in Psychiatry – Module One'.

2 Table adapted from American Psychological Association and Jansen, 'Reframing Psychology for the Emerging Health Care Environment'.

3 S. Mayor, 'Mindfulness Based Therapy Is as Effective as Antidepressants in Preventing Depression Relapse, Study Shows', *The BMJ*, 22 April 2015: https://doi.org/10.1136/bmj.h2107 (accessed 10 August 2023).

8

1 W. P. French, 'The Mountains of Mourne', All Poetry: https://allpoetry.com/The-Mountains-of-Mourne (accessed 9 August 2023).